The Democratic Party
in American Politics

The Democratic Party in American Politics

Ralph M. Goldman
SAN FRANCISCO STATE COLLEGE

The Macmillan Company, New York
Collier–Macmillan Limited, London

To the most powerful precinct organization
in the world: Joan, Peter, and Meg

First Printing

Library of Congress catalog card number: 66–14203

THE MACMILLAN COMPANY, NEW YORK
COLLIER–MACMILLAN CANADA, LTD., TORONTO, ONTARIO

PRINTED IN THE UNITED STATES OF AMERICA

Acknowledgments

Public expressions of gratitude are a fine art to which this note will obviously be a modest contribution. Particular thanks go to Nelson W. Polsby, series editor, and Robert J. Patterson, of The Macmillan Company, for making available the opportunity to engage in this labor of love. Although never hesitant to lower the editorial boom, both demonstrated once again their substantial patience and competence in dealing with this manuscript. A long overdue debt of gratitude is partially met with thanks to my former assistant, Alice E. Robinson, of Maryland, for helping build the reservoir of data from which much of this material was drawn. My colleague Eugene Weinstein, of San Francisco State College, and my wife Joan read the manuscript at various stages and gave me valuable literary and analytical advice. As usual, there is no one to whom I can pass any blame for what is in this book.

R. M. G.

Contents

CHAPTER 1

One Party Among Many

MEETING IN BALTIMORE, Maryland, during the second week of May, 1840, several hundred politicians decided to give their organization a new name: the *Democratic Party*. Officially, the meeting was the third national convention of the Democratic-Republican Party. The rechristening marked the beginning, in name at least, of the modern national Democratic Party.

Organizationally speaking, the party, as a national entity, was already eight years old. Historically speaking, the Democratic Party's antecedents reached back into Colonial life.

This was a political organization that helped conduct a great revolution, shared in the inauguration of a new nation, served as its first loyal opposition, safeguarded the nation's democratic institutions even during its one-party monopoly (1804–1824), and, under Jackson, modernized the political system by making the Presidency the most representative office in the land.

This was a political organization that would, during the 1850's, keep the parts of a dividing nation together for nearly a decade longer than could otherwise have been expected. It would survive an era of leaderlessness during and following a catastrophic Civil War, and for more than half a century thereafter would gather together the discontented on the farms, in the factories, in the mines, and among the recently arrived to these shores. This was the political organization that would manage the affairs of the nation during two world wars and during the worst economic crisis of modern times.

For sixty years a majority party, for seventy a minority party, and for the most recent thirty years again the nation's majority organization, the Democratic Party may claim to be the oldest and most persistent organizing influence in American life. For that matter, the party may also claim to be one of the oldest surviving organizations of any kind in human history.

Theories About Parties as Social Organizations

In the modern world there is hardly a nation among the more than one hundred that exist that lacks at least one political party; many nations have two or several.

In 1840, however, political parties as a type of human organization were rare. England had its Whigs and Tories, whose significance had only recently been augmented by the electoral reforms of 1832. In the United States there were the Democrats and the newly organized Whigs. Nearly everywhere else in western Europe there were popular clubs, secret societies, philosophical societies, and parliamentary groupings—but nothing organizationally identical with the nationwide legislative and electioneering organizations of the United States and England.

One hundred years *earlier* in England and the United States, parties were little more than temporary political groupings and parliamentary factions. Political parties as distinctive human organizations, in the modern sense, simply did not exist.

In many respects, the political party has been to the organization of political life what the corporation has been to the systematization of economic life. A much older organizational form than the party, the corporation became a vital instrument of large-scale economic cooperation early in the nineteenth century. The political party became an instrument for large-scale political cooperation around the middle of that century. Both types of organization soon flourished in the United States to a degree unmatched elsewhere.

What attributes distinguish the political party as a type of social organization? Theoretical and technical speculation on this matter has been wide-ranging.[1] Parties have been characterized as "social groups," "associations," "institutions," "systems," and "organizations." When we examine the definitions for these terms, it becomes evident that all share some reference to numbers of human beings communicating with each other about their political goals and the coordination of their respective efforts in attempts to achieve those goals.

Experts have also discussed the distinctiveness of parties on the basis of (1) types of people that belong to parties, (2) types of effort or activity to which party members devote themselves, and (3) types of goals that partisans characteristically seek to achieve.

In speaking of *types of people,* it is common for experts to refer to the differences between party leaders and followers. Parties are said to have an inner core of leaders surrounded by an outer circle of rank-and-file followers. Another definition tells us that we can recognize a political party by the fact that it includes nominees for public offices and is supported by voters in elections.

---

[1] A good survey may be found in Neil A. McDonald, *The Study of Political Parties* (New York: Random House, 1955).

Then there are those who focus upon the presumably distinctive *types of effort* or activity engaged in by party members. According to one definition, a political party is any organized group that manages the operations of governmental bodies. According to another, parties serve as brokers and mediators in reconciling the competing interests of groups in a community. Still another views mobilization of the electorate as the primary activity of parties, at which time party leaders engage in highly intensive communication efforts called *election campaigns*. A fourth defines parties as educators of the populace on matters of public policy. Still another point of view suggests that the distinctive activity of political parties is its nominations for public offices.

From another perspective, political parties are said to be distinguished by the *types of goals* or future states of affairs that they envisage. Thus, when an organization endeavors to create an entirely new system of government or accomplish a fundamental reorganization of the society as a political community, it is called an *ideological* or *revolutionary* political party. A party is described as *nondoctrinal* or *pragmatic,* on the other hand, when it seems interested in little more than capturing control of public offices. *Programmatic* is the name given to those parties that seem mainly preoccupied with bringing the demands and policy recommendations of divergent groups in the community into some kind of coherent platform or program. Finally, political parties are sometimes placed on a hypothetical conservative-liberal spectrum according to how much they seem to want the future to be the same as or different from the present.

A Brokerage Theory of Party Politics

One venerable theory of politics views politicians as *brokers* among groups and factions in the political community, making *deals* or consummating transactions. As expressed by Edmund Burke,[2] this brokerage function is of pervasive significance:

. . . All government, indeed every human benefit and enjoyment, every virtue, and every prudent act, is founded on compromise and barter. We balance inconveniences; we give and take; we remit some rights, that we may enjoy others. . . .

Sir Henry Maine [3] was even more explicit:

[2] Edmund Burke, *Speech on the Conciliation of the Colonies* (1896), pp. 67–68.

[3] Sir Henry Maine, *Popular Government* (1886), p. 30.

. . . The process of cutting up political power into petty fragments has in him [the political leader] its most remarkable product. The morsels of power are so small that men, if left to themselves, would not care to employ them. . . .

Transactional theories of political and social behavior have excited much interest in recent years. Such theories seem particularly appropriate for an understanding of the behavior of party politicians.[4] What the transactional approach suggests, succinctly, is that human beings exchange nonmaterial as well as material things. In typical economic activity, one person gives money or goods in exchange for another person's goods. In social exchanges, neighbors exchange favors, discussants trade ideas, colleagues give deference in return for advice, even lovers are active tradesmen.

In political exchanges, the consummation of which makes party politicians the busiest brokers in modern political communities, we also find many familiar deals being made: public economic resources are traded among competing interest groups; appointive offices are given for campaign support; during extensions of the suffrage or reapportionments of representation, political power is cut up, as Sir Maine describes it, into "petty fragments"; "balanced tickets" are composed, and so on.

The "best deals" are those in which all political interests come out of the exchange feeling satisfied, by their own standards, that they have received a *fair share* of the *political currency* being traded. The most successful party leader is the one who negotiates these transactions with sufficient skill so as to leave the greatest number of his constituents feeling "adequately" satisfied.[5]

What are some of the political currencies that are typically exchanged in political transactions? By *currencies* we, of course, mean the particular political media that make up the substance of political deals. At first glance it is fairly easy to recognize at least three types of political currency: the material type, the decisional type, and the positional type.

MATERIAL CURRENCIES. A substantial portion of governmental activity involves the allocation of *public* economic resources among

---

[4] Peter M. Blau, *Exchange and Power in Social Life* (New York: Wiley, 1964); George C. Homans, *Social Behavior; Its Elementary Forms* (New York: Harcourt, Brace and World, 1961); Ralph M. Goldman, "The Political Context of Arms Control," *Journal of Conflict Resolution* (September, 1963), pp. 618 ff.

[5] For another version of this process, Anthony Downs, *An Economic Theory of Democracy* (New York: Harper, 1957), Chap. 2.

the members of the community. The *commodities* of the governmental economy—such as public funds, public goods, public services, and public credit—have long been recognized by party politicians as a basic political currency. In advanced and modern communities, public commodities are perhaps what politicians trade with most frequently. Thus, taxation, budget preparation, and the uses of public monies are an almost constant concern. Party leaders discuss regularly in the economic planks of their platforms and in the economic programs that they promise to implement through legislation and administrative action if elected exchanges of public commodities such as these.[6]

DECISIONAL CURRENCIES. Politicians are invariably concerned about the distribution of shares of prerogative in the collective decisions of the community.

Who shall participate in those community decisions? The history of the suffrage laws is by and large the story of one group after another (nonpropertied persons, women, Negroes, and so on) gaining participation in the nation's electoral process.

What specific part of the collective decision prerogative shall be placed in the hands of each participator? An equal part of all the votes? A weighted proportion? A veto? Apportionment systems and vote-counting plans have become numerous and varied.

On what issues may politicians act in the name of the community? Every time a new function is assigned to the government, a new prerogative is placed in the hands of a public official and hence subject to the influence of party leaders. Friends of this tendency call it an extension of public services, whereas opponents call it government intervention. There are some issues, however, which Americans have clearly specified as none-of-a-politician's-business; the Bill of Rights does nothing less than *deny* governmental participation in such topics of personal choice as religious affiliation, communication and association with others, privacy of one's domicile, and right to bear arms.

POSITIONAL CURRENCIES. When organizations, including governments, are created, positions and offices are also brought into being. Such positions usually are given a name, certain duties, and certain decisional prerogatives. Each aspect of this process is politically negotiable: the creation of the organization of which the position is a

---

[6] A special type of public commodity, used under special conditions, is *armaments*—that is, public funds, goods, services, and credit employed to destroy, damage, or otherwise disrupt the normal operations of life and property.

part; the naming of the position; the assignment of duties to it; the assignment of prerogatives. The relationship between person and office is called an *incumbency*.

Modern political parties are constantly at work seeking to fill elective governmental offices or distribute as patronage the available appointive public offices. The selection of public officers has been a fundamental concern of politicians since the Greek thinkers first speculated about this problem. With the arrival of representative governments and popular voting systems, the selection of principal public officers became a matter for collective decision by representative assemblies or by mass electorates, under the guidance of party politicians—that is, experts in working out deals utilizing the incumbency currency.

Early congressional caucuses and later national nominating conventions became the American marketplaces for the trades and coalitions that enabled leaders and factions within each major party to more or less unite upon a single national ticket and platform. Much of the trading included not only the presidential and vice-presidential nominations but also prospective incumbencies in Cabinet offices. Platform fights usually revolved around prospective policies regarding public commodities—for example, the use to which public monies would be put; the economic interests to be favored by tax policies; the services to be performed under public auspices; the uses to be made of public credit.

We leave to the reader the interpretation of the innumerable transactions that will be reported in this account of the Democratic Party. It will become evident, too, that the Democrats have produced many of the most skillful political brokers in American history.

The Many Democratic Parties

A primary objective of party organizations is to capture control of governmental organizations. If there is no governmental organization, parties will try to create one; hence parties have a profoundly important role to play in new nations. If there are many governmental organizations, as in the American federal system, there will also be many party organizations reflecting that structure. Thus, in the United States, the major parties are as federal as the governmental system. There are local parties, state parties, and national-level parties.

The term *national level* is used here in lieu of *national* because parties at the federal level of government also reflect the division of that governmental organization into several elective parts. Therefore, at the national level, we find the congressional and the presidential wings of the party.[7] If we look more closely from an organizational point of view, we notice that the congressional party is in fact a party-in-the-Senate and a party-in-the-House. The presidential party has several semiautonomous organizational units: the political staff of the President; the national party chairman; the national committee; the national convention; the presidential campaign organization. Quite apart from all of these is the party-in-the-electorate, that special coalescence of voters who act on election days upon choices that invariably have profound consequences for all of these party agencies put together.

In American party politics, these many party agencies are semi-autonomous, capable of engaging in actions relatively independent of each other. Each party agency concentrates upon a different aspect of the political process. Each has a formal membership of its own, although overlapping membership is not uncommon. The degree of influence exercised by particular units varies according to formal arrangement, temporary political conditions, or the political personalities involved. Each recruits its leadership independently of the others. Each has a distinct constituency.

This account of the Democratic Party, therefore, will be organized to highlight the many local, state, and national-level parties that, together, become the Democratic Party. At the national level, we shall give particular attention to the story of the congressional Democrats on the one hand and the presidential Democrats on the other, noting the many situations in which they have united in common cause or divided upon some significant factional ground.

Throughout, we shall watch the forebearers of the Democratic Party evolve into modern Democrats. We shall see Democrats fight with other Democrats as well as with their opposition in the other party. We shall see how Democratic leaders have served as brokers for the nation and its many interests, trading available political currencies so as to build a governing consensus upon the widest possible distribution of satisfactions among all the people.

[7] Analyzed in some detail by James M. Burns in *The Deadlock of Democracy* (Englewood Cliffs: Prentice-Hall, 1963).

CHAPTER 2

Grass Roots and Building Blocks

LOCALISM has been a basic component in the organization and development of the Democratic Party. Local caucus clubs, committees of correspondence, and the Sons of Liberty were the immediate forebearers of the Tammany societies and the Democratic societies from which Madison and Jefferson built a national opposition party. Precinct and ward organization was the foundation upon which were built city machines and courthouse rings. The Democratic Party has never been far removed from the voter in his own home, group, and community. Democrats have been inveterate grass rooters.

In Colonies and Confederation

Even before the reign of George III began in 1760, American colonists were dividing among themselves into local cliques, caucuses, and electioneering committees for the purpose of mobilizing votes in the selection of public officers and the adoption of public policies in their town meetings and legislative assemblies. In the colony of Massachusetts, for example, this division saw the rise of a Court Party friendly to the royal governor and a Country Party comprising the same kinds of small shopkeepers, craftsmen, and laboring people that were then being drawn to the Whig Party in England.

One of the first of urban political machines, the Caucus Club of Boston, under the leadership of Deacon Samuel Adams and his son Sam, became a major component of the Country Party. The Caucus Club in fact became the prototype of similar electioneering organizations elsewhere in the colonies during this period. A primary objective of these clubs, soon to be known as *patriotic societies,* was to capture seats in the legislatures of those colonies that had such a body, there to make felt their opposition to royal economic measures.

One of the most significant immediate reactions to the British Stamp Act of 1765 was the capture of the Massachusetts House of Representatives by the Country Party, putting Sam Adams into the position of clerk of that body. For a decade Sam Adams used the prerogatives of this clerkship to encourage the organization of local patriotic societies in other colonies.

As these local *caucuses* spread and gained control of legislatures, they found themselves also in command of legislative committees of correspondence; these were the standing committees responsible for reporting official activities to sister assemblies throughout the colonies.

The committee of correspondence first became an extralegal instrument of revolution on November 2, 1772, when Sam Adams successfully pushed through a petition to form one at the town meeting of the city of Boston. Within two years this Boston Committee of Correspondence was in touch with more than three hundred towns in Massachusetts alone and with similar committees as far south as Charleston, South Carolina. In 1774, when the royal governors of North Carolina and New Hampshire dissolved their colonial assemblies, the members were reconvened on the initiative of their respective committees of correspondence. Similarly, when a shipment of tea in Boston Harbor on December 16, 1773, was destroyed, the Boston Committee of Correspondence was able to project that local skirmish into a continental movement.

Other activities of the committees of correspondence revealed their similarity to modern parties. They held regular meetings in many localities, consulted with similar committees in their vicinity, prepared political matter for use in the press and in pamphlets, coordinated the development of local and continental political policy proposals, promoted committee organizational efforts in surrounding localities, and solicited local citizen support for the continental cause. The committees of correspondence were indeed the precinct organization of the Revolution.

The Continental Congress came to rely heavily upon local committees of correspondence for the sinews of the Revolution, particularly since many of the colonial governments were either opposed to or divided on the issue of seeking independence. Washington's army suffered the same impoverishment that a modern political campaign might if it depended entirely upon volunteers and the Dollars-for-Democrats type of fund raising—enough to keep going but insufficient for a clear-cut victory.

Had it been a stationary war, it is doubtful that Washington could have accomplished the military mission. But there was tenacity among its personnel and friends among local committees of correspondence. The Continental Army, sometimes running away from and sometimes circumventing the British, kept constantly on the move, refreshing its resources with the help of committees of correspondence at different localities, exciting the more lethargic local citizens by direct contact with the great revolutionary effort, and moving on rapidly before their welcome had worn thin. In a real sense Washington's was a beggar army, engaged in a political as well as a military campaign, passing the hat on a continent-wide scale.

With victory and independence came unanticipated problems of self-government. The nationalists in Congress became the prime movers in calling and conducting the Constitutional Convention. When a proposed Constitution was brought forth by that convention, the nation became embroiled in what amounted to a constitutional referendum. In selecting delegates to the state ratifying conventions only about 5 per cent of the total population became involved in one way or another, but under the limited suffrage of that day, this was a substantial participation.

The Democratic Societies Under the New Union

With adoption of the Constitution the Federalists moved into control of the offices of the new national government they had done so much to create. At the local level, however, anti-federalism subsided only long enough to give the first Washington administration a chance to mobilize itself and the nation. The Hamilton-Jefferson policy and personal disagreements in the Cabinet and the division of congressional forces into "Hamiltonians" and "Madisonians" soon led to the reactivation of old local political organizations, stimulated the organization of new ones, and led to local coalitions called the Democratic-Republican Party.

In the period 1789–1792 local party organization was uneven in the nation at large. But Colonial and Revolutionary electioneering experience brought relatively trained hands to the task of building parties capable of naming slates and delivering popular majorities. In some places, notably New York and Pennsylvania, committees of correspondence continued to nominate and campaign. In other places, however, the absence of organization led to a multiplicity of candidates for particular offices. Coping with these types of situations came to be a primary objective of the Democratic and Tammany societies that emerged between 1792 and 1800.

At first, many of these societies had little interest in nominating slates or managing election campaigns. Their initial motivation was to discuss the issues that deeply divided the new nation and, frequently, to express opposition to Federalist policies. The first such society to appear was organized by German-Americans in Philadelphia: The German Republican Society. On April 13, 1793, the *National Gazette* announced this Society's formation and published its first announcement, which might still serve as an excellent founding declaration by some modern civic group:

> In a Republican government it is the duty incumbent on every citizen to afford his assistance, either by taking part in its immediate administration or by his advice and watchfulness, that its principles may remain uncorrupt; for the spirit of liberty, like every virtue of the mind, is to be kept alive only by constant action. It unfortunately happens that the objects of general concern seldom meet with the individual attention which they merit and that individual exertion seldom produces a general effect; it is, therefore, of essential moment that political societies should be established in a free government, that a joint operation may be produced, which shall give that attention and exertion so necessary for the preservation of civil liberty.[1]

Late in May a Norfolk and Portsmouth Republican Society appeared in Virginia. A third society, organized soon after in Philadelphia, became one of the most influential. The Philadelphia Society was located at the seat of the national government, acquired many national political leaders among its members, and aggressively urged the formation of similar societies in every section of the nation. In many ways, it was the Boston Caucus Club reincarnate. Eleven other societies were organized during 1793, twenty-four during 1794, and three during 1795.

Certain characteristics of these post-Revolutionary popular organizations were clearly indigenous, traceable to the pre-Revolutionary committees of correspondence and Sons of Liberty. These included the straightforward practice of association for public action, extensive use of committees in their organizational structure, and the key role assigned to their committees of correspondence. So effective did these American action groups seem to be that the English began to imitate the organizing technique during the 1780's, and not long after, the French Jacobin Clubs followed suit.[2]

The societies of Philadelphia were in fact the first to argue that "political parties" were legal and essential instruments of balance in the rough waters often encountered in pursuit of liberty. President

[1] Quoted from Eugene P. Link, *Democratic-Republican Societies, 1790–1800* (New York: Columbia University Press, 1942), p. 6.
[2] *Ibid.,* pp. 20–24.

Washington did not share this conception. In his message to the Third Congress on November 19, 1794, he went out of his way to condemn the activities of "certain self-created societies," implying that these groups had been responsible for the Pennsylvania Whiskey Insurrection.

In general, these societies were city or county political associations. They usually held monthly meetings in courthouses and other public edifices. With the degeneration of the outdoor mass meeting as a nominating technique, these societies began to assume nominating functions. All had committees of correspondence which kept in touch with societies in other counties and states. During most of this formative decade, the Democratic-Republican societies directed their electioneering efforts to winning local and congressional objectives. Aaron Burr, a Tammany leader, introduced the device that came to symbolize modern organizing proficiency: the card index of voters' names.

Even after Jefferson became President and as the Federalists began to slip into oblivion, local Democratic-Republicans persisted in their grass roots efforts. Systematic observation of party preferences among the local citizenry became standard local organizational procedure. A letter from Alexander Wolcott, Collector of the Port of Middletown (Connecticut), to fellow partisan William Plumer describes the technique.

Have each county leader appoint a manager for each town in his county, wrote Wolcott. Each town manager should appoint district managers who would list the names of all male freemen, taking pains to divide this list into "decided Republicans," "decided Federalists," "doubtful." These district managers, continued Wolcott, were to get all eligible freemen to take the necessary oath at registration time and furnish these freemen—particularly the friendly ones—with "votes" (the prepared paper ballots of that day). Each town manager was to be assigned dates for forwarding their estimates of voter preferences to county managers who, in turn, were to consolidate and forward them to the state manager. In addition, every manager was to be active in the circulation of campaign literature and, on election day, in reporting his own estimates of local election returns.[3]

Between 1800 and 1830 several factors profoundly influenced the shape of local Jeffersonian Democratic affairs. Despite the War of 1812, scattered depressions, and incessant frontier engagements, the

[3] December 5, 1805, *Repository,* Vol. III, William Plumer Papers, Library of Congress.

country in general was experiencing an era of peace and prosperity. Population growth and its exodus to the West kept older eastern city and county parties preoccupied with the identification of new voters even as they lost old voters.

It did not take long for the politicians of the new West to appreciate that all rifle-bearing men were equal before the hardships and Indian skirmishes of the frontier. Hence, new western states, as rapidly as they became organized, gave the vote, great instrument of equality, to all white men of legal age (twenty-one years in the Anglo-Saxon tradition).

The egalitarian suffrage ideas filtered eastward soon enough. There workingmen's groups and fraternal associations among the foreign-born began to press for removal of property ownership and tax payment as suffrage requirements. By 1830 universal white manhood suffrage had radically altered the electoral environment in the older states. This was evident from the introduction of the penny newspaper (newspapers had been expensive upper-class media previously), the resurgence of local Democratic organizations (many of which had fallen dormant during the one-party Era of Good Feeling), and the attendance of the muddy-booted mob at the inaugural of General Andrew Jackson, a popular hero who was to transform the Presidency into an agency of the mass electorate. It was Jackson who attracted many of the newly enfranchised voters into the Democratic Party, giving older city and county party units a new lease on life and the less experienced Democratic organizations at the frontiers a large infusion of blood.

Tammany as a Prototype

No account of local Democratic Party politics can fail to take a long look at the Tammany Hall of the nineteenth century. To speak of city political "machines" and "bosses" was to conjure up images of Tammany and its grand sachems. Rare was the political reformer who failed to condemn his opponent for being a "Tammany boss." Yet, after his long career of tilting at the machine-driven windmills of urban politics, the great muckraking newspaperman Lincoln Steffens conceded that no political system functions without organization and leaders who can understand the special kinds of transactions that are made in politics. In this sense, urban bosses and machines in general merit recognition as important contributors to American self-government.

The Tammany Society, founded in 1789, originated as a fraternal and benevolent association of veterans of the American Revolution. Whereas the Order of the Cincinnati attracted officer veterans, Tammany brought together the privates and veterans of enlisted rank. Whereas the Cincinnati moved along with the Federalist cause, Tammany became part of the Jefferson-Madison alliance. Aaron Burr, the first "boss" of Tammany, led that organization to its first great political triumph in national politics; Tammany carried New York for the Jefferson-Burr ticket in 1800, much to the consternation of the previously dominant Hamilton organization.

Over the next five decades the Tammany organization grew, as did New York City and the nation. Its alliance with Van Buren helped carry New York for Jackson in 1828. Its factional divisions during the 1840's and 1850's reflected the national party's growing schism between North and South. As wave after wave of immigrants arrived from Europe, they found that the great American melting pot seemed to consist mainly of New York City, with Tammany grand sachems in charge of cooking the ingredients.

William Marcy Tweed and his henchmen captured control of the organization in 1863 and, through it, control of the New York City government. By graft and theft from the city treasury, the Tweed ring has been estimated to have cost New York as much as $75,000,000. Tweed's use of the loot was, to add insult to skullduggery, of the most ostentatious sort, including a reported $700,000 wedding for his daughter.

From within the Tammany organization, however, John Kelly, Richard Croker, and the Scannell brothers fought a steady battle to free the organization and the community from Tweedism. By 1871–1872 they were joined by many eminent Democrats, including Samuel J. Tilden and Abram Hewitt.

With the overthrow of Tweed, Tammany experienced several years of reduced influence. But under the direction of "Honest John" Kelly and his successor, Croker, the organization reestablished its mastery of the incessantly shifting New York City political environment. Croker's biographer, writing in 1901, was moved to declare: "Tammany Hall, as a 'machine,' is perfect." [4]

Within the "pyramid of Tammany power" at the close of the century were some 90,000 members and more than 220,000 other voters. A *captain* for each city block, another *captain* for each voting

[4] Alfred Henry Lewis, *Richard Croker* (New York: Life Publishing Co., 1901), p. 156.

precinct, a *leader* for each of thirty-five assembly districts, a finance committee of five selected by the leaders, and, finally, the chairman of the finance committee, that is, the *boss*—this was the organizational structure that spread out of Tammany Hall on Fourteenth Street, a million-dollar edifice, into thirty-five assembly district clubhouses, each valued at approximately $100,000. The expressive language of Croker's biographer is worth quoting at length. He describes some of Tammany's operations *circa* 1900.

To conduct a campaign Tammany Hall spends about three hundred thousand dollars. This money is given out the night before an election; each "leader" having his share. The wage and the number of election workers are fixed. There are to be ten men in each voting precinct to wear the badge and get the people to the polls. These receive five dollars each or fifty dollars to a precinct or over seventy thousand dollars for this one item alone covering the entire town. Then there are carriages to bring the lame, the halt, and the blind. There are halls to rent, and fireworks to purchase, and stands to put up, and trucks to hire for "orators" in the three or four weeks of a canvass. Told and counted, the over-all expense clambers to three hundred thousand dollars. This sum is not hard to get. Contributions come from every quarter; some of them secret and not caring to be known.

. . . There are hundreds to whom a part of their subscriptions is returned as "too large," or "more than the organization needs."

Following an election, what money is left is generally given to a charity or to some cause of worth. Within the past four years there have in this manner gone, to the poor of this town, forty thousand dollars; to the cause of Cuba, forty thousand dollars; almost as much to the Galveston sufferers; almost the same sum to rear a monument to Parnell, and to pay the mortgage on the Parnell estates in Ireland and save them to the family of that dead liberator. Tammany keeps no books; there's no way of discovering who gives how much; the funds are banked in the name of a treasurer who acts as secretary to draw checks and aid the work of the finance committee.

That is the money, and in a sense, the military side of Tammany Hall. There is still another, and it is this latter which makes it wellnigh impregnable in local affairs. Tammany is a political organization one day in the year; it is a charitable, benevolent, fraternal organization three hundred and sixty five.[5]

It is in the latter role that we see the boss in his principal function as a broker. In an era when employment agencies and union hiring halls were rare and the United States Employment Service nonexistent, unemployed laborers by the score and the hundreds could be found applying for work every morning at the doorstep of their

[5] *Ibid.,* pp. 156 ff.

Tammany captain. The Tammany leadership was geared to refer these unemployed to builders, contractors, and nearly every other business enterprise in the city. Satisfaction with these deals depended heavily upon regular and competent job performance by the Tammany stalwarts. In return, Tammany could do much for cooperating builders, contractors, and other business enterprises. Through its influence in the city's administrative departments, Tammany could facilitate petitions of one sort or another, favor a Tammany contractor's bid over others, allocate public funds and credit in a manner favorable to friendly interests in the community, provide police protection, and so on.

Tammany also rendered service to countless individuals facing minor penalties in the city's police courts. A Tammany representative was usually present to pay the small fine. In gratitude, the petty criminal, thereby escaping an unhappy period of imprisonment, would presumably "vote right" at the next election. Nor was this a haphazard procedure in which an obligated citizen might renege or forget to vote; the records of the city courts served as a kind of reckoning book of those who had become politically obligated to the Tammany organization.

When well led, Tammany could also channel the expression and resolution of local dissatisfactions. Efficient "machines" were always sensitive to the complaints of the disorganized, the underprivileged, the unemployed, and the newcomers. The boss who knew his business would always be out in the field ready to greet some newly organized community interest as it came over the horizon. If business leaders or the wealthier taxpayers registered serious dissatisfaction with the costs of local government, the astute boss would either retrench or remind them of the even higher costs of police protection from riots, unemployment, vandalism, and public relief to the distressed.

Operating the equivalent of a community political supermarket in which countless small transactions took place from day to day, Tammany (and similar machines) became "perfect" in the word of Croker's biographer; its leaders exhibited skill in managing "the store" and satisfying all the customers.

As the New York County organization, Tammany, in more recent decades, provided leadership to the Democratic organizations in the four other counties of New York City. So long as Manhattan (New York County) remained the most populous and the richest, Tammany remained the most powerful. But the surge of population into Brooklyn (Kings County) and the Bronx (Bronx County) produced such challengers to Tammany hegemony as Frank V. Kelly of Brooklyn and Edward J. Flynn of the Bronx. Tammany, in the 1940's and 1950's, was never the same.

A Sampler of Bosses and Machines

The honor roll of Democratic bosses is filled with the names of men who were able to maintain and operate the governments of major urban communities during periods of dramatic change and in the absence of other leadership. "Good" bosses became "bad" when the civic costs of their operations became onerous in the opinion of the citizenry. "Good" machines were left unassailed when they charged no more than seemed a "fair price" for their services.

In the quaint language of Richard Croker's biographer, the cities and the nation derived great good from the much maligned machines of the nineteenth century.

. . . It [the machine] is in perpetual arms political; and it acts as coastguard of American institutions. The "machine" makes captive the ignorant, the anarchistic, and the unrepublican, as he lands. It ties him hand and foot with its discipline and makes him harmless. As a suppressive influence, moving for public order and to the subjection of what else might be a mob spirit and rise to become those small first gusts of violence which unchecked conflate as riots, the "machine" is to be extolled.

In either the theory or the ethic of politics the "machine" cannot find defense; in the practice of politics, and peculiarly in cities, the "machine" cannot find dispense. That is because both theory and ethic deal with man as he should be, while practice deals with man as he is. And hence the "machine." [6]

As other organizations and other leaders began to compete with the machine, antibossism became a struggle for control of political functions in the community. As a result of these contests, covert "wheeling and dealing" was transformed into overt public business. The relief of the economically distressed, for example, was removed from private management by some local wardheeler to public management by government-supported relief agencies, unions, and public employment agencies.

Still among the major currencies of local politicians are the allocation of municipal construction contracts, the disposition of many petty criminal cases, and, perhaps above all, the local management of the growing number of federally supported community programs such as

[6] *Ibid.*, pp. 149–150.

urban redevelopment, civil and military defense operations, anti poverty programs, and so on. Factors such as these produced sub stantial political pressure for creation of the office of Secretary o Urban Affairs in the President's Cabinet.

NEW JERSEY.   In 1897, a twenty-one-year-old lad named Frank Hague won his first election as constable of Jersey City. In a city rife with political gangs and extraordinarily rough election-day methods, Hague rose to be mayor in 1918, elected his first governor in 1919, and by 1925 had a 100,000-vote Hudson County bloc with which he frustrated all attempts to overthrow him. He held sway until 1949.

It was in the late 1940's that Hague ran up against the rising in fluence of the New Jersey Congress of Industrial Organizations (CIO), an alliance of anti-Hague county and regional leaders, and a loss of allies in the presidential party. Hague's regime had become the most costly on a per capita tax basis in the country. The following decade was spent by other New Jersey Democrats reducing that cost by reducing Hague's power.

MASSACHUSETTS.   Boston Democratic politics was for generations rooted in its ward leadership: a city-wide boss never emerged. Until the late 1920's the two most powerful organizations were the Hen dricks Club of the Eighth Ward, for forty years dominated by Martin Lomasney, and the Tammany Club, which served as the vehicle for the rise of James M. ("Jim") Curley. Sometimes as allies, more often as competitors, and always in changing coalitions with lesser ward organizations, these two wards produced into the 1940's whatever cohesion Boston and Massachusetts Democrats seemed to achieve. From these organizational roots have come such party eminences as Maurice Tobin, the Fitzgeralds, their descendants the Kennedys, Speaker John J. McCormack, and innumerable others.

TENNESSEE.   Ed Crump rose to the top of Memphis politics around 1903 and remained there for more than half a century. Un challengeable in Memphis, where he was four times its mayor, his alliance with a county machine—the Sheriff Birch Biggs gun-toting organization—in eastern Tennessee enabled him to dominate that state's politics for nearly as long.

World War II brought back to Tennessee a wave of politically conscious veterans as competent with guns as the Biggs machine. The New Deal and the Fair Deal also left a trail of young liberals. The emergence of Estes Kefauver as a presidential prospect in 1952, over Crump's objection, together with the difficult role a border state must play in the North-South dispute within the Democratic Party, compelled the Crump influence to retreat to its major base, Memphis, by the mid-1950's.

ILLINOIS.   Chicago, during the 1920's, was a scene crowded with gangsters (e.g., Al Capone), corrupt business magnates (e.g., Samuel Insull), and purchasable party machines. During the 1920's, a period of Republican ascendancy, two Democrats pulled together a minority coalition that came to be known as the Kelly-Nash machine. The man who perfected Democratic organization in the city, however, was a Czech named Anton J. Cermak, who masterfully developed winning coalitions among the many nationality groups—Polish, German, Russian, Italian, Swedish, Irish, Czech, Austrian, Lithuanian, and Greek—enough to carry him into the office of mayor in 1931. Cermak was killed in an assassination attempt upon President-elect Franklin D. Roosevelt in 1933, leaving the city's Democratic leadership in the hands of Kelly and Nash.

Nash died in 1943, and the aging Mayor Kelly promoted Colonel Jacob Arvey into the county chairmanship. Eager to modernize the party's image, Arvey sought out, nominated, and helped elect Adlai E. Stevenson and Paul H. Douglas as governor and United States senator, respectively, in 1948. Governor Stevenson appointed as director of his Department of Finance the former minority leader of the Illinois Senate, Richard J. Daley.

A lawyer and Cook County leader since 1935, Daley succeeded Arvey as Democratic county chairman in 1953. In 1955, Daley took over as mayor, to give Chicago a unique combination of old-style machine politics and new-style reformism. A scandal in the police department was handled by appointing a University of California professor of criminology as superintendent of police. A decade's immigration of southern Negroes that put unprecedented strains upon the city's housing, education, and employment facilities was met with some $400 million in housing projects and $500 million in super-highway construction. Racial tensions were minimized by the party's assiduous attention to population shifts. So well has the Chicago "store" been kept that local Republicans and Democrats alike have fallen in line behind the Daley banner.

Other Local Party Developments

In this brief sampling of what Democrats have done at the local community level, many topics have of course been omitted: e.g., rural machines, the impact of organized crime, organized labor.

RURAL MACHINES.   One traditional American attitude, originating in the early days of the republic when this was predominantly an agricultural nation, is that farmers and things rural are somehow more pure, wiser, and in general closer to God. The notion of a rural machine has seemed almost sacrilegious. Yet, rural machines there have been and continue to be. The Democratic variety, in the form of courthouse rings, has been found mainly in the townships and counties of the South.

Perhaps the principal difference between rural and city parties is the amount of land space between members. Otherwise, the county *courthouse gang* is the equivalent of the *city-hall heelers*. Although they may have country-style names, rural political practices—in organizing, campaigning, brokerage of political currencies, patronage, and so forth—are basically the same as those in the urban centers, even though less noticed in political writings and in the public mind.[7]

ORGANIZED CRIME AT THE GRASS ROOTS.   In the United States as in no other nation the apprehension of criminals is a responsibility assigned to local governments. We have already noted how readily the urban machine may bring the petty criminal under obligation to it by simply bailing him out, paying his fines, or providing legal counsel.

In the nineteenth century, particularly the latter half, petty criminals, either as individuals or as local gangs, were a common urban phenomenon and problem. Cities very often had inadequate police protection, leaving nationality and other urban groups to their own procedures of self-protection. Cities were crowded with unemployed and unskilled workers, leaving these to their own ingenuity in acquiring money and other economic resources, often by theft and related activities. Local politicians, as community brokers, could hardly ignore such ever-present segments of their constituencies, particularly when elections were themselves occasions for fraud and violence.

In the twentieth century, particularly during the Prohibition era, crime, like other aspects of American life, became highly organized. National and statewide gangs emerged. Criminal syndicates took on the characteristics of large industrial holding companies. Before long, local branches of syndicates, political parties, and governments were meshing and accommodating to each other. Mayor "Jimmy" Walker

---

[7] For a study that revealed examples of rural party machines, mostly Democratic, see V. O. Key, Jr., *Southern Politics in State and Nation* (New York: Knopf, 1949).

of New York City, for example, symbolized the high life of the city during Prohibition and watched over a shadowy alliance of Tammany politicians, city officials, and syndicate criminals. This pattern continues to be found from time to time. Sometimes it seems that the gangsters are running the politicians; sometimes the politicians seem to be running the gangsters.

ORGANIZED LABOR IN LOCAL POLITICS. The New Deal gave unprecedented stimulus to union organization in this country. As a consequence, labor, like other organized interests, developed a concern for party politics and election outcomes. Wages and working conditions, labor discovered, were inextricably related to the general costs of education, medical care, credit, food, housing, and so on. And these costs were profoundly influenced by public policy. Electing friendly policy-makers to the Presidency, Congress, and local offices became a major preoccupation of organized labor, especially during the 1950's.

Union officials and members found that they could perform many of the activities—registering voters, helping candidates campaign, raising funds, getting voters to the polls—ordinarily left to the parties. The unions began to adopt one or another political strategy, depending on local conditions: (1) supplement the campaign of friendly candidates, with money, publicity, volunteeers, and so forth; (2) where it could operate as a balance-of-power influence, throw its resources to the party or candidate that makes the best bid; (3) challenge the party regulars in the primaries; (4) engage in a year-round take-over of party positions and organs; (5) develop alliances with other groups in order to influence party decisions.[8] Often, union locals served the Democratic cause in the absence of party locals.

THE DEMOCRATIC CLUB MOVEMENT. The boss and the machine began to disappear or change civic roles as other agencies and organizations assumed competing functions. Sometimes the bosses, like Daley of Chicago, adapted successfully. Sometimes, as in the case of Carmine DeSapio of New York, they tried but did not succeed. DeSapio's defeats, it should be added, were at the hands of a "reform" candidate of the Democratic club movement.

In the 1950's the club movement had many of the impulses and characteristics of the turn-of-the-century reform movements. Both were constituted by citizens of somewhat better education, income,

[8] For a thorough treatment of these strategies, see Fay Calkins, *The CIO and the Democratic Party* (Chicago: University of Chicago Press, 1952).

and philosophical motivation. Both were antimachine in approach The contemporary clubs differed from the earlier ones, however, in that they committed themselves to stay *within* the party organization rather than try to influence the party from *outside*. Club members become much more involved in ideological controversies, often discussing public policy issues longer and louder than most older party regulars find bearable.

By 1954, in California, neighborhood clubs throughout the state joined to form the California Democratic Council, which endorses state candidates and issues and campaigns actively in their behalf. By 1957 there was a Democratic Federation of Illinois. In New York there began in 1959 a New York Committee for Democratic Voters. Other club movements have emerged in Michigan, Kansas, Pennsylvania, and Colorado.

The Democratic club movement is a grass roots attempt to develop new modes of participation for new kinds of participants. The club movement may also prove to be a method for legitimizing the development of an important form of subgroup within political parties, namely, factions. Competitive factionalism is to the vitality of party organizations what competitive parties are to the vitality of a nation.

The Ultimate Grass Roots: Democratic Voters

If all the poor people are Democrats and all the rich people Republicans, then it should follow that Democrats would be in office all the time—for there are surely more poor people than rich ones.

This might be the case if the basic premise were correct—that is, if the people divided between poor and rich and adopted political parties accordingly. However, approximately 90 per cent of the voters consider themselves middle class in the United States. The psychological line between poor and rich becomes thin and permeable. Consider, too, that the poorer the voter, the less likely he will get to the polls to vote at all. If that prospective nonvoter also tends to be a Democrat when he does vote, his staying home is one vote less for the Democratic ticket, or the equivalent of two votes for the Republicans (the one that would have cancelled his vote and the one needed to win).

In order to specify clearly what is involved in the changing characteristics of the Democratic voter and in his predisposition to be more of a nonvoter than his Republican counterpart, the following table was drawn together from various sources. The table tells what percentage of all the voters were Democrats in a particular category and in a particular election year. It also tells, in the figures within parentheses, what proportion of the voters in the particular category did not vote that year. For example, in 1948, 53 per cent of the male voters were Democratic, but 31 per cent of all males eligible to vote failed to do so.

From the table we are able to see some of the social, economic, ethnic, religious, and other characteristics of the "typical" Democratic voter. We are also able to see to what extent these characteristics have changed in their typicalness from election to election.

1. A larger proportion of men have tended to be Democrats, except in 1948 and 1964 when the reverse was the case. (Obviously, sex difference is not a reliable way to look for a Democrat.)

2. Two thirds and more of the nonwhite population (mostly Negroes) have supported the Democratic Party, with a high of 94 per cent in 1964.

3. More grade school people than those who have been to high school and more high school people than those who have attended college are Democrats.

4. The less the occupational skill of the voter, the greater is the chance that he is a Democrat. Notice how much the farmers have fluctuated between the parties.

5. The older the voter, the less likely he is a Democrat.

6. Among religious groups, Jews have been overwhelmingly Democratic, Catholics next, and Protestants least.

7. The lower the family income, the greater the chance that the voter is Democratic.

8. From its former position as the most Democratic section of the country, the South has become the least Democratic.

9. Italian and Polish nationality groups have been the stanchest supporters of the Democratic Party.

But even though three out of every five potential voters in the United States identify themselves as Democrats what joy over these figures can the party have if one of these three is the one most likely *not* to vote. The figures within parentheses reveal the dilemma. These are the proportions of all voters in each category who failed to vote. Notice how vulnerable the highly Democratic categories are.

The Democratic and Nonvoting Portions of the Nation's Electorate, 1948–1964

Characteristics	1948 Dem.	(NV)	1952 Dem.	(NV)	1956 Dem.	(NV)	1960 Dem.	(NV)	1964 Dem.	(NV)
Sex:										
Male	53%	(31%)	47%	(21%)	45%	(20%)	52%	—	60%	—
Female	58	(41)	42	(31)	39	(33)	49	—	62	—
Race:										
White	55	—	43	—	41	—	49	—	59	—
Nonwhite	64	—	79	—	61	—	68	—	94	—
Education:										
College	30	(21)	34	(10)	31	(10)	39	—	52	—
High school	55	(33)	45	(20)	42	(26)	52	—	62	—
Grade school	65	(45)	52	(38)	50	(40)	55	—	66	—
Occupation:										
Professional and business	28	(25)	36	(12)	32	(15)	42	—	54	—
White collar	47	(19)	40	(19)	37	(21)	48	—	57	—
Skilled labor	63	(29)	—	(26)	—	(28)	—	—	—	—
Manual labor	67	(50)	55	(40)	50	(47)	60	—	71	—
Farmers	66	(58)	33	(33)	46	(26)	48	—	53	—
Age:										
21–29	ca. 62	(ca. 40)	51	(ca. 28)	43	(ca. 31)	54	—	64	—
30–49	ca. 54	(ca. 30)	47	(ca. 22)	45	(ca. 24)	54	—	63	—
50+	ca. 48	(ca. 33)	39	(ca. 22)	39	(ca. 22)	46	—	59	—
Religion:										
Protestant	53	—	37	—	37	—	38	—	55	—
Catholic	64	—	56	—	51	—	78	—	76	—
Jewish	—	—	—	—	—	—	71	—	91	—
Income:										
Under $2,000	63	(54)	55	(47)	—	(48)	—	—	—	—
$2,000–2,999	66	(39)	46	(32)	—	(40)	—	—	—	—
$3,000–3,999	52	(26)	47	(24)	—	(31)	—	—	—	—
$4,000–4,999	47	(25)	49	(17)	—	(25)	—	—	—	—
$5,000+	32	(18)	34	(12)	—	(17)	—	—	—	—
Region:										
East	—	—	45	—	40	—	53	—	68	—
Midwest	—	—	42	—	41	—	48	—	61	—
South	—	—	51	—	49	—	51	—	52	—
West	—	—	42	—	43	—	49	—	60	—
Nationalities:										
Irish	—	—	47	—	—	—	—	—	ca. 55	—
Italians	—	—	60	—	—	—	67	—	75	—
Poles	—	—	50	—	—	—	68	—	74	—
Germans	—	—	40	—	—	—	—	—	ca. 50	—

Sources: American Institute of Public Opinion (Gallup), release of December 21, 1964; Harris Poll, in *Newsweek* (November 2, 1964); A. Campbell et al., *The Voter Decides* (Evanston: Rowe, Peterson, 1954); V. O. Key, Jr., *Politics, Parties and Pressure Groups* (5th ed., New York: Crowell, 1964), p. 587; L. Harris, *Is There a Republican Majority?* (New York: Harper, 1954).

1. When women are more Democratic than ordinarily (as in 1948), they also are most likely *not* to vote.

2. The less educated (predominantly Democratic) are also the ones who go to the polls *least often*.

3. *Nonvoting* is greatest among the least skilled and lowest in income (both types predominantly Democratic).

4. Although precise figures are not given in the table, nonwhites (predominantly Democratic) are three to four times more likely than whites to be *nonvoters*.

The apparent Democratic Party advantage—that is, if we take seriously voters' self-identifications (three in five calling themselves Democrats)—proves to be an unreliable measure when we examine who actually gets to the polls. And it is at the polls that the votes count.

These data for only five elections hardly take into account the complexities of long run trends in party preference. However, the figures do suggest certain difficulties that the party encounters over the years as the characteristics of voters generally, and Democrats particularly, change. For example, as the proportion of the electorate in the higher educational categories increases, may we expect a decline in Democratic voting strength? As the occupational skills and economic affluence of the voters increase, will the lesser categories, now predominantly Democratic, become thinner? Will these trends be compounded by the fact that the more educated, the more skilled, and the more affluent are also more likely to cast their ballots?

In the days before public opinion polls, local group and party leaders were the principal reporters of change among Democratic voters. Local leaders of different religious, nationality, racial, occupational, and income groups were in frequent communication with local party leaders—sometimes making demands, other times offering support, always transacting deals. Group demands were thus translated into precinct and ward dimensions, which, in turn, were added up into city, state, and national party strategies for producing consensus in the most pluralistic society in the world.

Today, with somewhat different sources of data, party leaders continue to face the task of adding up a consensus. Polls may help national leaders keep track of changes in the general characteristics of Democratic voters. New party leaders may strive valiantly to remain as representative of the new electorate as former leaders were of the old. Yet, an essential part of the job must, today as before, remain in the hands of the party at the grass roots. It is only at the grass roots that political transactions may be attuned to voters' characteristics, voters may be helped to the polls, and group demands may be converted into precinct and ward dimensions on election day.

CHAPTER 3

State Parties and Sectional Politics

ONE OF THE PROPOSALS for electing a President of the United States, presented at the Constitutional Convention, recommended that the choice be made by a conference of the governors of all the states of the Union. The proposal was rejected on grounds that it was contrary to the principle of federalism, which requires the states and the nation to remain sovereign in the respective areas of governance assigned them. Nonetheless, over the decades, state politicians sought other channels through which to influence national politics, and this they accomplished through the political parties.

Where Is the Hub of the State Parties?

The following table, showing what proportion of Democratic governors served as delegates to the Democratic national nominating conventions in selected years, suggests how one such party channel has evolved.

Democratic Governors Serving as Delegates to National Party Conventions, Selected Years *

Year	Governors	Delegates	Per Cent
1848	20	0	0
1860	20	1	5
1872	12	1	8
1884	25	4	16
1896	17	5	29
1908	20	11	55
1920	21	11	52
1928	21	9	43
1932	27	18	67
1936	38	23	61
1940	30	18	60

Democratic Governors Serving as Delegates to National Party Conventions, Selected Years *—Continued

Year	Governors	Delegates	Per Cent
1944	22	18	82
1948	24	15	63
1952	23	19	83
1956	27	20	74

* Paul T. David, Ralph M. Goldman, and Richard C. Bain, *The Politics of National Party Conventions* (Washington, D.C.: Brookings Institution, 1960), p. 98.

As the table indicates, governors did not come into their own on the national political scene until after the Civil War. Neither national party nominated an incumbent governor for President until 1876, at which time the Democrats chose Governor Samuel J. Tilden of New York, and the Republicans nominated Governor Rutherford B. Hayes of Ohio. The evolution of distinctive state-level party organizations was equally slow, and probably the two were concomitants of each other.

In the early days of the republic, statewide party organization was essentially an aspect of state legislative politics. The best known of the state political "machines" were the Richmond Junto in Virginia and the Albany Regency in New York. The Junto served as the operating hub of the "Virginia Dynasty"—Jefferson, Madison, and Monroe—which controlled the Presidency from 1801 to 1825. The Regency served as the springboard for Martin Van Buren's rise during the late 1820's as a key figure in the Jacksonian leadership, a founder of the modern Democratic Party and its titular leader into the mid-1840's.

That the focus of party politics outside of the national capital was in the state legislatures was in keeping with the antiexecutive, anti-centralization preferences of the colonists. It also reflected some of the basic governmental arrangements written into the Constitution. For example, the power to regulate elections and establish the qualifications of voters was given to the state legislatures. Presidential electors were to be named in the manner preferred by these legislatures, and through 1820 these bodies retained a substantial place for themselves in this process.

Eligibility to vote for members to the lower house of the state legislature was also a standard in the Constitution for voters for representative to the Congress. Selection of United States senators was left entirely to the state legislatures. When in 1913 the Seventeenth Amendment transferred that power from the state legislature to the electorate at large, a century-long decline in the power of these legislatures reached a low point.

The growth of state party organization outside the state legislatures during and after Reconstruction produced governors and United States senators who themselves became the bosses of powerful state machines. Political transactions were, after Reconstruction, no longer mainly conducted in the state legislative marketplace but, instead, began to depend upon the governor's or the senator's capacity to negotiate with the national party, with the President, and with powerful allies or adversaries in the United States Senate.

The Democratic Strongholds in the South

What have been the historic state strongholds of the Democratic Party? A long-run view of state party fortunes may be found in the following table, which indicates what proportion of the times each state voted in presidential elections it went to the Democratic nominee. The denominator of each fraction following the state's name indicates the number of presidential elections in which the state participated since it came into the Union. The numerator tells how often that state's voters went for the Democratic candidate between 1824 and 1964, the former date being the earliest with general popular participation in presidential elections.

Number of Presidential Elections in Which State Participated and Per Cent Times Carried by Democratic Nominee, 1824–1964

State	Democratic Wins/ Total Participation	Per Cent Democratic Wins
Hawaii	2/2	100.0
Arkansas	30/32	93.8
Texas	25/28	89.3
Alabama	31/35	88.6
Georgia	30/34	88.2
Mississippi	29/34	85.3
North Carolina	29/35	82.9
Virginia	28/34	82.3
South Carolina	20/25	80.0
Louisiana	27/34	79.4
Florida	21/28	75.0
Missouri	27/36	75.0

Number of Presidential Elections in Which State Participated and Per Cent Times Carried by Democratic Nominee, 1824–1964—Continued

State	Democratic Wins/ Total Participation	Per Cent Democratic Wins
Oklahoma	10/15	66.6
Tennessee	23/25	65.7
New Mexico	9/14	64.3
Kentucky	23/36	63.9
West Virginia	14/26	53.8
New Jersey	19/36	52.8
Montana	10/19	52.6
Idaho	10/19	52.6
Arizona	7/14	50.0
Utah	9/18	50.0
Illinois	18/36	50.0
Delaware	17/34	50.0
Alaska	1/2	50.0
Nevada	13/26	50.0
Maryland	17/36	47.2
New York	16/35	45.7
Wyoming	8/19	42.1
Washington	8/19	42.1
Colorado	9/22	40.9
Indiana	14/36	38.9
California	11/29	37.9
New Hampshire	12/36	33.3
Pennsylvania	12/36	33.3
Connecticut	12/36	33.3
Ohio	11/36	30.6
Rhode Island	11/36	30.6
Wisconsin	9/30	30.0
Nebraska	7/25	28.0
Michigan	9/33	27.3
North Dakota	5/19	26.3
Minnesota	7/27	25.9
Oregon	7/27	25.9
Massachusetts	9/36	25.0
Kansas	6/26	23.1
South Dakota	4/19	21.0
Iowa	6/30	20.0
Maine	7/36	19.4
Vermont	1/35	2.8

Thirteen states have gone Democratic in two thirds or more of the presidential elections in which they have participated. Seventeen states have gone Republican as often. Only twenty states appear, over the long run, to have been competitive two-party states, and only six of these of the fifty-fifty order.

In a glance, the table suggests the basis for the claims of southern Democratic politicians over the decades that the "heart" of the Democratic Party lies in their section of the country. Who can contest the fact that Arkansas, Alabama, Georgia, Mississippi, Texas, Virginia, South Carolina, North Carolina, Louisiana, Florida, Missouri, Oklahoma, Tennessee, and Kentucky have been more *consistently* Democratic in their national party behavior than any other states in the Union? By comparison, Democratic successes in, say, New York and Illinois have been far less "reliable," as some Democrats would put it.

However, southern claims have been diluted by other factors, for example, the changing population sizes of the states. Whereas Virginia, for example, was at first the most populous state in the Union, by 1812 it gave way to New York. And in the census of 1970, New York will give way to California. In a mass democracy such as the United States, politics is where the people are.

Perhaps the most critical qualification to be placed upon southern claims of special loyalty to the Democratic cause is that which is revealed by a comparison of party organization in competitive two-party states with those in one-party states. The preceding table shows Virginia to be a consistently one-party Democratic state and New York going Democratic only half the time. The organizational consequences of different competitive situations at the state level is well illustrated in the stories of Virginia and New York.

The Richmond Junto: A One-Party State

Most of us know Patrick Henry best for his great Revolutionary phrases ("Give me liberty or give me death!"). Most would be uncomfortable about including this patriot's name on a roster of powerful American state bosses. Yet, state boss he was—leader of a potent organization called *the Richmond Junto,* direct forbear of what is today called *the Byrd machine.*

The Junto had its roots in the Virginia Assembly, where Patrick Henry was the Anti-Federalist leader. So powerful was Henry that he was able to prevent James Madison's election to the Senate in the First Congress under the new Constitution; Madison went to the House of Representatives instead. Over the years Henry and his successors at the head of the Junto developed strong working alliances with fellow partisans in Kentucky, North Carolina, and Georgia, with effective ties into their local rural-agricultural organizations. These interstate alliances gave the Richmond Junto a major role in national politics for well over the first half century of the republic's history. The Junto was particularly powerful during the years of *the Virginia Dynasty,*—that is, the presidencies of Jefferson, Madison, and Monroe.

Modern Virginia has operated under the Junto-like organization of Senator Harry F. Byrd. Hal Flood, the Senator's uncle, and, later the Senator bound together the governor's office, the state compensation board, the county officialdom, the circuit judges, and local party officers into a closely knit machine under Byrd leadership. Nominations for elective office, distribution of appointive offices, salaries for officials at all levels of government within the state, and public services are all carefully managed in the interest of the state machine. "Yet," wrote Professor V. O. Key, Jr., in 1949, "the little oligarchy that rules Virginia demonstrates a sense of honor and aversion to open venality, a degree of sensitivity to public opinion, a concern for efficiency in administration, and, so long as it does not cost much, a feeling of social responsibility." [1]

The Virginia political environment has had two main attributes of particular importance for the Byrd machine: (1) relatively inconsequential competition from the Republicans, and (2) a low voter turnout. Throughout the 1920's, 1930's, and 1940's, less than 12 per cent, on the average, of the adult population voted in Democratic primaries. In the general elections for governor, however, the proportion hovered closer to 8 per cent. Republican inroads have mainly occurred in a few county organizations, one or two congressional districts, and in support of certain presidential nominees.

The problems of a party in a noncompetitive state are similar to those of any organization that controls an entire field. First, although it may resist the development of external competition, it must tolerate a limited amount of internal contentiousness among its adherents. Second, it must resist large voter turnouts, particularly at party primaries; the greater the number of participants, the higher the risk of dissident elements.

Third, the party in a monopolistic political environment can and must maintain ideological and policy simplicity, often as tests of loyalty to the machine. In Virginia, the policies of "white supremacy" and "balanced budget" have served this purpose for decades. Fourth,

[1] *Southern Politics* (New York: Knopf, 1949), p. 19.

in the absence of a well-organized adversary, the party monopoly must guard against political surprises, making it particularly wary that its political muscles may become flabby and its political judgment poorly informed. Fifth, a monopoly need not worry too much about elaborate organizational techniques for the articulation and negotiation of internal differences. In the last analysis, the buck could always be passed to the boss, in this case, Senator Byrd.

New York's Albany Regency: A Two-Party State

A very different set of working circumstances confronts a Democratic Party organization in a competitive two-party state such as New York. The following table, although limited only to turnout and popular voting for the Presidency, demonstrates several points.

First, the party cannot escape its competitive predicament; margins of victory are very frequently narrow (from 1 to 5 percentage points between the major parties), in fact, narrow enough to invite third-party activity.

Second, the party must press for its best possible voter turnout, as the New York percentages (from 56 to 92 per cent) indicate. This means a constant search for hidden reservoirs of unsolicited or uncaptured voters.

Third, the party must maintain a substantial ideological and policy sensitivity and adaptability, for the needs of the new or the uncommitted voters change rapidly and continuously. Fourth, because it must constantly face a well-organized adversary, the party in a competitive state must maintain an elaborate intelligence system lest it be surprised by events in the campaign and outcomes at the polls. Fifth, because it is inevitably a coalition of innumerable minority interests, the competitive-state party is constrained to invent techniques for hearing, negotiating, and compromising differences—that is, the marketplaces (committee, convention, and so on) for its brokers must be well designed and efficient.

Competitive interparty politics also invites competitive *intra*party politics. New York Democrats have had contentious factions from the very beginning. At first the battles were among the Clinton, Burr, and Tompkins factions. By 1821 Van Buren had firmly established the Albany Regency, which was for the most part the Democratic-Republican caucus of the New York state legislature. By welding together a coalition of Tammany and anti-Clinton elements, the Regency built the Bucktail faction.

During the 1830's and 1840's Barnburners fought with Hunkers within the party.[2] The Barnburners rested upon the support of farmer and labor groups, distrusted banks, and were actively hostile to the extension of slavery. Hunkers were strongly for promoting the interests of business and weak in their opposition to slavery. Eventually Van Buren led the Barnburners into the Free Soil Party, and the remaining Hunkers divided into moderate "Softshell" and conservative "Hardshell" factions.

The Softshell-Hardshell battles raged through the 1850's, with Horatio Seymour and Samuel J. Tilden working hard to reconcile them. During the Civil War, the party had its War and Peace factions. During the 1870's, factionalism took on a Reform versus the Machines coloration.

New York's Voter Turnout and Popular Vote Percentages in Presidential Elections, 1828–1964

Year	% Turnout *	Democratic %	Republican % †	3rd Party %
1828	—	51.0	49.0	—
1832	—	52.1	47.9	—
1836	—	54.6	45.4	—
1840	—	48.2	51.2	0.6
1844	—	48.9	47.9	3.3
1848	—	25.1	47.9	26.4
1852	—	50.2	44.9	4.9
1856	—	32.9	20.9	46.1
1860	—	46.3	53.7	—
1864	—	49.5	50.5	—
1868	—	50.6	49.4	—
1872	81.0	46.7	53.1	—
1876	92.0	51.3	48.1	0.2
1880	92.0	48.4	50.3	1.1
1884	89.0	48.3	48.2	2.1
1888	92.0	48.1	49.2	2.3
1892	85.0	49.0	45.6	2.9
1896	84.0	38.7	57.6	1.2
1900	85.0	43.8	53.1	—
1904	83.0	42.3	53.1	2.3
1908	79.0	40.7	53.1	2.4
1912	72.0	41.3	28.7	24.7
1916	72.6	44.5	51.5	2.7
1920	56.5	26.9	64.6	7.0
1924	56.3	29.1	55.8	14.6
1928	68.3	47.4	49.8	2.4

[2] See p. 51 for origin of these faction names.

New York's Voter Turnout and Popular Vote Percentages in Presidential Elections, 1828–1964—Continued

Year	% Turnout *	Democratic %	Republican % †	3rd Party %
1932	66.1	54.1	41.3	3.8
1936	72.6	58.9	39.0	1.6
1940	75.7	51.6	48.0	—
1944	72.7	52.3	47.3	—
1948	69.2	45.0	45.9	8.3
1952	68.3	43.6	55.5	—
1956	66.0	38.8	61.2	—
1960	67.0	52.5	47.3	—
1964	—	68.6	31.3	—

* Turnout is ratio of total actual vote cast to potential vote according to suffrage standards of the period. Potential votes for noncensus years are interpolated estimates.
† Includes National Republicans of 1828 and 1832, Whigs from 1836 to 1856, and Republicans thereafter.

The Tilden mantle was passed on to Cleveland in the 1880's and 1890's only to be contested by the Tammany and David B. Hill forces. These divisions were followed by Tammany versus the Wilsonians, until substantial unity was again achieved, as it had been under the Albany Regency, behind the leadership of Franklin D. Roosevelt and Herbert Lehman. In more recent years, Democratic factions have once again been berating one another.

And always there are the skillful Republican opposition, pivotal third-party movements, close election outcomes, high turnouts, the programmatic sensitivities, and sustained attention to organizational problems.

Recent Party Competition in the States

Such have been the histories of Democrats in Virginia and New York, the one a prototype of one-party politics and the other of competitive partisanship. Leadership and organizational problems in each are emphatically different from the other. But what is it like in the other states? Professor Malcolm E. Jewell [3] has examined the period 1947–1962 for patterns of party control of houses of the state legislature and the governorship. (Nebraska and Minnesota were omitted because they have nonpartisan legislatures; Alaska and Hawaii because of their brief terms as states.) He found that in the

[3] *The State Legislature: Politics and Practice* (New York: Random House, 1962), pp. 10 ff.

following states Democrats controlled the governorship and both houses throughout this recent period, with the minority's representatives never going over 20 per cent of the strength in either house: Alabama, Arkansas, Florida, Georgia, Louisiana, Mississippi, North Carolina, South Carolina, Texas, and Virginia. The same degree of party ascendancy, but with the minority sometimes achieving over 20 per cent of the seats, existed in Oklahoma and Tennessee.

Democrats always controlled both houses in Arizona, Kentucky, Maryland, and West Virginia, but did not always hold the governorship. In Missouri and New Mexico, Democrats controlled both houses most of the period 1947–1962 and the governorship at least half of the time.

In Nevada and Connecticut it was the state senate and in Rhode Island and Massachusetts the lower house that Democrats held during most of the period, with Democrats holding governorships most of the time in Rhode Island and Connecticut but only half of the time in Nevada and Massachusetts. Democratic governors faced hostile legislatures (both houses) in Michigan and Ohio during these years.

The most competitive states, in which neither party dominated the legislatures nor the governorship without potent challenge from the other party, were Pennsylvania, Idaho, California, Oregon, Montana, Washington, Utah, Colorado, and Delaware.

A somewhat different perspective is provided by Professor Paul T. David. In a tabulation of the voting in presidential and gubernatorial elections, giving each state its percentage weight in the Electoral College, he found a decided disappearance of one-party states, both Democratic and Republican, in the presidential voting, but a decline in one-sidedness of gubernatorial voting primarily among the Republican states.[4]

Categories of States *	Period 1896 to 1927		Period 1928 to 1956	
	President	Governor †	President	Governor
One-party Republican	50.0%	35.1%	1.5%	7.5%
Two-party leaning Republican	10.7	10.5	23.1	18.4
Two-party uncertain	10.3	16.4	23.4	33.0
One-party leaning Democratic	4.9	12.3	40.2	14.0
One-party Democratic	24.1	25.7	11.8	27.1

* States were classified in the one-party category when the party concerned was victorious in 80 per cent or more of the elections during the period; as leaning to one party when the party was victorious in 60 to 79.9 per cent of the elections; and as uncertain when neither party won more than 60 per cent of the time.

† Based on the period 1901–1927.

[4] "The Changing Political Parties," in John R. Owens and P. J. Staudenraus, *The American Party System* (New York: Macmillan, 1965), p. 436.

What does the future hold for Democratic Party development at the state level? The following speculations may point up some of the tasks that lie ahead for state-level Democrats.

1. There is a clear and probably irreversible trend toward tighter competition between the parties at the state level. For such competition, state Democrats will need to develop more flexible and durable state party agencies and attend more closely to the recruitment of skilled political talent.

2. Since popular election of United States senators was established in 1913, the senator has been the principal competitor of the governor in evolving state party organizations. The senator has had certain advantages. For example, he is more likely because of his location at the news center of Washington to receive the publicity that is the lifeblood of politicians. Further, while the governor is struggling valiantly but never too successfully with growing state fiscal problems, the senator is among those who are dispensing some of the major resources of the nation, for today Congress is indeed the principal national political marketplace.

Thus, the future is likely to see gravitation of state party organization toward senators rather than governors. Already countermeasures are being taken by the governors, whose collective political activities at the annual Governors' Conference are increasing in volume and significance.

3. After decades of state legislative malapportionment, the current reapportionments are likely to give state Democrats a temporary advantage in numbers of seats captured. This advantage, however, is likely to be reduced by the factionalism that comes with holding substantial but not overwhelming majorities.

For those who may be overly concerned about the future of the federal system in this country, the prospect of a more vigorously competitive state party politics offers much hope, as stronger and more responsive state parties and governments contribute to the vitality of each state and the nation as a whole.

CHAPTER 4

The National Party's Emergent Decades

IN THE EARLIEST STAGES of their development, political parties find their most natural habitat in legislative assemblies. The numerous membership of such bodies, particularly when chosen from distinct and independent constituencies, could hardly function without the party-like working alliances and coalitions that are a major preoccupation of party politicians in democracies, particularly the United States.

Despite many swings in political ascendancy between the executive and legislative branches of American national government, the members of Congress have succeeded in making a major place for themselves as individuals and as partisans in the affairs of the nation, the states, and the local communities. Each member of Congress belongs to a national body, elected under rules and conditions determined within his home state, and beholden, at least theoretically, to the voters in his district. The special combination of national-state-local ties has produced special subgroups of Democratic Party leaders: the party-in-the-Senate and the party-in-the-House, or, together, the congressional party.

In most representative democracies, political parties tend first to emerge as alliances among members of the legislative assembly, then as captors of the chief executive offices of the government, and finally as contestors for the electoral support of the voters, historically in about that sequence. Often, particularly in parliamentary systems, the chief executive officer is himself a member of the legislative assembly—for example, the British Prime Minister. American representative democracy has been different, however, in that parties functioned as electioneering organizations long before they became captors of the chief executive offices of the government.

The Colonial governors were not elective. The Articles of Confederation provided for no chief executive. When the office of President of the United States and the Electoral College that was to choose him were created in the Constitution, the Founding Fathers started an experiment that has produced the most powerful yet most institutionally constrained office in the world's history. If President Washington viewed his office as something of a constitutional monarchy standing above partisan politics, no President in modern times, to paraphrase Woodrow Wilson, can escape serving as leader of his party in its campaigns and its management of the affairs of the government.

While the exact confines of the *presidential party* are not well delineated, there are fairly clear locations to which one customarily looks for presidential party leaders and activity: the Presidency itself, and the President's most recently defeated opponent; the staff of the Office of the President; the Cabinet; the national chairmanship of the party and its national committee; in an increasingly significant way, the Vice-Presidency; the large array of "presidential politicians" (that is, state and local partisans who become particularly active only in the presidential years); the peculiar coalitions of organized interest groups that endeavor to advance their programs by influencing the national platforms and by maintaining access to prospective presidents; and, last but hardly least, the national conventions.

In the early decades of the republic, however, there was little clarity about the composition and location of the national-level organs of the party. In fact, there was little certainty about the organization of the national party itself. The Madisonian coalition in Congress came to be called "Jeffersonians," then "Democratic-Republicans." Democratic-Republicans fell apart into personal followings, a major one of which was the "Jacksonian." The Jacksonian Democratic-Republicans became, organizationally, the modern Democratic Party.

With these transformations went various shifts in the early centers of party influence at the national level: from the House where Madison led and King Caucus emerged, to the Presidency where Jackson and Van Buren built the first presidential wing; from the Presidency, to the Senate where Clay, Calhoun, Webster, Walker, Cass, Slidell, Douglas, and other pre-Civil War titans held sway. Not until the administrations of Cleveland and Wilson did the presidential wing of the party again enjoy the influence it did in the Jackson-Van Buren eras.

Madisonians and Jeffersonians in Caucus

Article I of the Constitution provided an initial distribution of sixty-five seats in the House of Representatives. The Senate consisted of twenty-six members. According to the population distribution in 1788, the largest number of House seats went to Virginia. As the most eminent Representative from the largest state, James Madison held a "natural" seniority from the outset. Madison, as it turned out, also became the leader of the first *loyal opposition* in the American system.

Most leading members of Washington's Administration conducted themselves as though they were participants in a parliamentary system of government. President Washington assumed the style of a "Whig king." Most important, however, was Hamilton's behavior. Hamilton, following William Pitt's example, assumed responsibility for formulating and promoting legislative programs. It had been Pitt's opinion that one of the ministers should hold the principal place in the confidence of the King and that he should also be "the person at the head of the finances." Hamilton endorsed this theory and converted the office of Secretary of the Treasury into a prime ministry from which he sent forth the Administration's legislative program.

Nominally, the Federalists held all 26 seats in the Senate and 53 of the 65 seats in the House during the First Congress. In the Second Congress there were ostensibly 17 Federalists among the 30 senators and 55 Federalists among the 69 congressmen. The fact is that party-like patterns of voting hardly existed during the first three sessions of Congress.

With the Fourth Congress (1795–1797), however, came a hardening of party lines. This came with the development of the party caucus in Congress and with a new mood of impatience with moderate or independent congressmen. In the Fourth Congress, about 66 per cent of the Federalist and 74 per cent of the Democratic-Republicans voted together with great consistency. By the Seventh Congress (1801–1803) some 81 per cent of the Federalists and fully 94 per cent of the Democratic-Republicans exhibited partisan voting patterns.

The party caucus was a major instrument in achieving such cohesion. The first congressional caucus took place on April 2, 1796, when the Democratic-Republicans gathered to discuss the controversial issue of appropriating funds for the implementation of the Jay Treaty with England. Division of popular opinion on the treaty coincided with Federalist predispositions toward England and Democratic-Republican sympathies for France. The treaty passed the Senate by the minimum constitutional margin, 20-10. On the appropriations questions, the Democratic-Republican majority in the House decided to organize themselves for the ensuing floor debate and caucused to do so.

There followed a month-long debate in the Committee of the Whole. The decisive vote resulted in a 49-49 tie, broken in favor of the treaty by the chairman of the Committee of the Whole, a Democratic-Republican whose political career ended shortly thereafter. Madisonian congressmen, in a round of letters to their constituents, castigated party members who had deserted under pressure. The notion of party loyalty in congressional politics was thus established, and the caucus became its implementing instrument.

Thereafter, Congress became physically and politically the most convenient location for consultation among Jeffersonian politicians. Pending legislation, state and local voting trends, cooperation and coordination of national political campaigns, and eventually preferences for President and Vice-President became grist for the caucus mill. Thus in 1796 the Democratic-Republican caucus tightened its lines in support of Jefferson for President. Jefferson became Vice-President in that year. Once elected President in 1800, Jefferson continued to use the caucus as his primary political tool for advancing his legislative program and assuring that the succession would pass to Madison.

It was an era in which even Presidents acknowledged the supremacy of Congress among the branches of the national government. Jefferson, Madison, and Monroe deferred accordingly. With the disappearance of the Federalist Party from the halls of Congress and the arrival of the Western "Warhawks," led by Henry Clay, this presidential deference increased. By 1810–1820 the outsized Democratic-Republican majorities had degenerated into the personal factions of Henry Clay, John Quincy Adams, John C. Calhoun, Daniel Webster, William H. Crawford, and others.

The following table summarizes the one-party character of congressional politics between 1801 and 1824—that is, during the terms of the Seventh to Eighteenth Congresses. The table shows the Federalist opposition's rising percentage "deficit" in portion of seats held.[1]

[1] An "opposition deficit" is one half the difference between the majority's percentage and the principal minority's percentage of the total available seats. For example, if the majority held 65 per cent of the seats and the principal minority 35 per cent, the difference between the two would be 30 per cent. One half of the 30 per cent, or 15 per cent, represents the proportionate shift in seats necessary in order for the minority to *tie* the majority. The opposition deficit figure, therefore, is a convenient measure of relative partisan strength.

| House of Representatives | | | Senate | |
Majority Party	Opposition Deficit in Seats	Session of Congress	Majority Party	Opposition Deficit in Seats
DR	15.5%	7th	DR	6.0%
DR	22.5	8th	DR	24.0
DR	32.0	9th	DR	29.0
DR	33.0	10th	DR	32.0
DR	16.0	11th	DR	32.0
DR	19.5	12th	DR	33.0
DR	11.5	13th	DR	25.0
DR	14.0	14th	DR	18.5
DR	26.5	15th	DR	27.0
DR	35.0	16th	DR	30.5
DR	36.0	17th	DR	42.0
DR	38.0	18th	DR	42.0
Pro-Adams	1.5	19th	Pro-Adams	6.0
Pro-Jackson	6.0	20th	Pro-Jackson	8.0

The dramatic drop in opposition deficit in both houses of the Nineteenth Congress reflects the work of Senator Van Buren as he gathered support for Andrew Jackson's presidential candidacy and, coincidentally, built the foundations for the modern Democratic Party. In the Twentieth Congress (1827–1829) the Jacksonians held the upper hand.

Emergence of the Democratic Presidential Party

The first semblance of an organized presidential party may be found in the political correspondence of Thomas Jefferson and James Madison, giving advice and coordinating decisions regarding actions to be taken in the Electoral College. By 1796 the Democratic-Republican congressional caucus took on this work. Agreement in the caucus was not always easily reached or unanimous. The followers of the Clintons of New York were repeatedly rejecting caucus choices. By 1816 the Crawford followers gave James Monroe a hard battle for caucus endorsement. The main thrust of the Jackson campaign of 1824 was its anticaucus position. What is commonly referred to as *the Jacksonian Revolution* in presidential politics was in fact the success with which the Jackson men brought to an end the era of outright congressional selection of Presidents.

Throughout the nation, particularly along its frontiers, restrictive suffrage requirements were being removed, and hundreds of thou-

;ands of newly enfranchised citizens stood ready to follow a new national hero. In addition, the economic panic of 1819 struck farmer and worker alike, and these economic "underdogs" were more than receptive to Jackson's subsequent campaign against the "interests." A defender of the nation, Jackson also appeared as a protector against the disunionists and nullifiers who seemed eager to destroy the Union. A partisan fighter, Jackson nonetheless seemed to be above party organizations, which were still suspect among the citizenry-at-large. Above all, Jackson was a frontiersman whose plain manner and speech symbolized the contrast between the new electorate and the political aristocracy of New England and Virginia that seemed to have a stranglehold upon King Caucus, hence the Presidency. The legend of his victory against the British at New Orleans established General Jackson as the principal outsider with substantial presidential prospects.

This setting made of Jackson the leading political actor of the period. However, in 1822 when the Nashville *Gazette* proposed Jackson's name for the Presidency and the Tennessee legislature added its endorsement, General Jackson was, organizationally speaking, little more than a local favorite son. Jackson might well have remained a favorite son had it not been for the political and organizing skill of a small group of devoted Tennessee politicians. These men converted Jackson's military fame into enduring political alliances across the nation, established party organs where none had been before, and everywhere paved the way for popular reception of the hero himself. Their most notable achievement was the creation of a coalition with Martin Van Buren, leader of New York's Albany Regency and long a supporter of William Crawford for the Presidency.

In 1824 Van Buren's genius for political organization was already widely recognized. Forty-two years of age, father of four, a widower, the "Little Magician" had gained a reputation for pulling victories out of very deep political hats. Born to extreme poverty, he never lost his identification with working people. If Jackson's name was the catalyst, Van Buren was the political chemist who could make the most of the elements at hand. Van Buren welded together the Albany Regency, the Richmond Junto, and the hardy group of Tennessee politicians to inaugurate the Jacksonian Era. In 1832 the Jacksonians became incorporated, in a literal sense, as a presidential party by holding the first Democratic-Republican national convention in Baltimore.

In Congress, Van Buren carefully developed issues and tests that gave heart and strength to the new Jacksonian alliances. He worked diligently to alter state procedures for popular selection of presidential electors; in New York, state legislative selection was replaced by popular election in 1828, thereby adding over a quarter of a million new voters to the million then composing the presidential electorate. Van Buren also did all that he could to help transform the *United States Telegraph* into the leading national Jackson newspaper.

Extension of the suffrage and intensification of presidential politics were accompanied by organizational activity at the local level. Ward committees and county committees met frequently, developed political information, endorsed local candidates, and campaigned with increasing intensity and skill during this period. In the more rural localities, school-district and township committees did similar work. At the state level, general corresponding committees and state committees concerned themselves more and more with the standard activities of political parties: the conduct of political rallies, distribution of literature to the voters, the selection of representatives to various political conventions, the collection of funds, the prevention of fraudulent voting, the printing of ballots, the preparation of lists of eligible voters, and the measurement of voter preference.

The House of Representatives remained, from the 1790's through the 1820's, the principal arena of national politics. In 1811, Henry Clay became Speaker and held that position six times through 1825. The crystal clarity of his influence was missed by no one when Clay presided, particularly when the House denied the Presidency to Andrew Jackson in 1824 and gave it instead to John Quincy Adams.

That situation is summarized in the following table. The popular vote was Jackson's. In the absence of an Electoral College majority, however, the decision went to the House, in which Speaker Clay sat as master. There he transformed Adams' popular minority of 31.9 per cent into a House majority of 54.2 per cent.

Distribution of Voting Strength in Presidential Election of 1824

Candidate	Popular Vote	Electoral College	House Vote
Jackson	42.2%	37.9%	29.2%
Adams	31.9	32.2	54.2
Clay	13.0	14.2	—
Crawford	12.9	15.7	16.6

Jackson returned to Tennessee from Washington reiterating at every stop the charge that Clay had purchased a Cabinet position (Secretary of State) by making a President. Before another quadrennium had passed, however, Jackson had been renominated and elected to the Presidency.

President Jackson was the first to retain a personal political staff. The Kitchen Cabinet enabled the President to consider the partisan implications of his acts and, perhaps more important, maintain communication lines with his allies in Congress and in the state organizations. While the men in the Kitchen Cabinet changed over the years, their general characteristics tended to be the same; they were men who understood how to evaluate and influence the voting behavior of legislators and the electorate. Van Buren was constantly in touch with the members of this staff, which included Jacksonian managers in Congress, the President's private secretary, the editor of the Administration's official newspaper, the leader of the Jacksonian party in New Hampshire, and others.

The Kitchen Cabinet proposed strategies and tactics in the political battles undertaken by the President, but it was Jackson who chose the battleground. This same staff arranged for the first national nominating convention and developed the propaganda used in the ensuing campaigns. Its "chief of staff" was always Van Buren, whether as Senator, Secretary of State, or Vice-President.

The coalition of factions over which Jackson presided as party leader was at all times an uneasy one. Northeastern Democrats tended to support the protective tariff and oppose western demands for large expenditures on internal improvements. States' rights southerners stood for tariff reduction and the principle that any state in the Union could nullify any federal law—in this case the tariff—with which it was in basic disagreement. Western frontier Democrats wanted cheap land, usually at the expense of the Indians, transportation and other internal improvements at federal expense, and low-interest loans.

A major objective of the Crawford (Richmond Junto) and Van Buren (Albany Regency) collaboration was the frustration of Vice-President Calhoun's presidential ambitions. The Calhoun–Van Buren rivalry soon pervaded all aspects of national politics but manifested itself particularly in Calhoun's insistence upon tariff reduction and the implementation of his theory that any state could interpose its authority to nullify a national law.

By April, 1831, Jackson initiated steps to remove the Calhoun supporters from his Cabinet. Van Buren led off with his own resignation in order to give the President a free hand to reorganize, and shortly thereafter Jackson nominated him by interim appointment to be ambassador to England, pending the return of Congress. Van Buren departed for England. The vote on confirmation in January, 1832, was, as expected, controversial and produced a 23-23 tie. Vice-President Calhoun exercised his prerogative and broke the tie to vote *against* confirmation. The affront to Jackson was clear.

The one issue that reduced presidential politics in 1832 to simple pro-Jackson and anti-Jackson dimensions was the bank issue. The second Bank of the United States was, in effect, a private monopoly handling the public currency. Aside from the suspicion with which Jackson and Van Buren viewed bankers in general (a consequence of their respective frontier and working-class backgrounds), both also understood the partisan implications of the existence of the national bank. The bank, through its many branches in most of the states could, during campaigns, serve as a potent political machine. The bank retained Daniel Webster as its counsel, expanded or contracted credit to suit its purposes, and served the political causes of Henry Clay and other National Republicans. When the bank applied for recharter in 1832, a petition that was granted by Congress, Jackson clamped down his veto and added a fighting message. The veto of the bank bill set a basic orientation to Democratic positions on banking and currency that is felt to this day.

During Jackson's second term, alliances among party leaders became increasingly volatile even as debates on national issues became more and more inflammatory. Shortly after the presidential election of 1832, the Nullifiers of South Carolina, through the state legislature controlled by them, called a special state convention to issue an Ordinance of Nullification. This proclamation stated that the federal tariffs of 1828 and 1832 were to be considered null and void insofar as enforcement within South Carolina was concerned. Unionist Democrats in the state held a separate convention and condemned the ordinance. On the same day, Jackson issued a proclamation declaring the national government sovereign and indivisible. No state could refuse to obey the law, he declared, and no state could leave the Union. Over the next three decades this was the issue that destroyed the Whig Party, divided the Democratic Party, and propelled the nation into civil war.

Decade of Division

The Jackson Administration submitted a Force Bill to Congress which would permit military measures if necessary to preserve federal interests in South Carolina. During this crisis Henry Clay's compromise, soon accepted by all adversaries, provided for gradual reduction of all tariff duties to the revenue level in exchange for abandonment of the protectionist principle. The compromise also produced a Force Bill which empowered the President to use armed forces to execute federal law in South Carolina. When South Carolina repealed its Ordinance of Nullification with respect to the tariff, however, it at the same time nullified the Force Act.

Differences among Democrats during the 1830's tended to reinforce sectional loyalties. The strains between pro-Calhoun Nullifiers and pro-Jackson Unionists in South Carolina had repercussions elsewhere in the South. Abolitionist positions on slavery were beginning to win important adherents among northern Democrats and aggravate the suspicions of southern Democrats. Political support for the annexation of new territories hinged mainly on whether the new territory lay in the free Northwest or the slaveholding Southwest. Soon the slavery problem was riding close upon the heels of the extension of the frontier.

As these issues became increasingly intense during his second term, Jackson straddled and postponed. Thus, when the issue of annexation of Texas came up in 1835, he delayed action until after the election of 1836. Vice-President Van Buren, who was elevated to the Presidency in that election, could be thankful for this postponement, but it hardly alleviated his difficulties over the long run.

The winning coalitions that Van Buren had gathered on behalf of Jackson became increasingly difficult to hold during his own tenure. This was particularly evident in the growing breach between the Albany Regency and the Richmond Junto. The Democratic Party had been developing other astute professionals eager to gain control of the initiatives available to the presidential party, and some of these became Van Buren's most ardent adversaries. The "Little Magician," however, was a professional politician not easily persuaded into retreat or retirement.

Possibly the first great "adversary" was the Panic of 1837. Economic depression dominated Van Buren's entire Administration. The

Panic was preceded by speculation in canal and land investments, crop failures, and unsettled farm credit arrangements. Jackson's disbursement of public funds, previously deposited in the National Bank, among state banks had further encouraged speculation. Van Buren's response to the crisis was, in the main, a plan to establish an independent treasury system, but to little avail. The nation's economy never did recover while he was in office.

Slavery was another deep wedge into the Democratic ranks. John Quincy Adams, former President turned Representative from Massachusetts, presented a petition on December 12, 1837, calling for the abolition of slavery in the District of Columbia. Six days later the southern members walked out en masse to deliberate upon their line of conduct.

Meanwhile, in the Senate, Calhoun introduced a series of resolutions defining the character of the federal system and the rights of the "slave states" under it. Several of the resolutions indicated that the right of holding slave property was a state matter guaranteed under the Constitution. Another resolution placed the question of abolishing slavery in the District of Columbia and the territory of Florida (the only slave territory at the time) into the hands of Congress, but then proceeded to forbid such abolition for "high expedient reasons." Tactically, Calhoun offered a masterful deal, avoiding the slavery issue and making a natural affirmation of congressional prerogative.

Southern leaders pressed Van Buren for his views. He took the position that a state had jurisdiction over slavery only within its own boundaries and that the Constitution did not give Congress the power to interfere either in the states or in the District of Columbia. Rather than let the slavery question become a clear-cut factional issue, nearly all Democrats united behind a strange alliance between Van Buren and Calhoun in defeating the petition for the abolition of slavery in the District of Columbia. The issue of slavery, however, did not go away, and the party's action on this petition set a precedent that became increasingly difficult for it to follow in later years.

As the 1840 presidential election approached, the new Whig Party gathered itself with all the skill available to Thurlow Weed of New York, its new master politician. The Whigs set Henry Clay's aspirations aside, nominated General Harrison, the hero of Tippecanoe, and enlisted John Tyler, a Virginia Democrat, as his vice-presidential companion. The Democrats, on their part, renominated President Van Buren unanimously but indicated the great split within the party by failing to agree upon a vice-presidential nominee. Subsequently, three entered the race.

The singing and marching "Tippecanoe and Tyler, too" campaign defeated Van Buren by a very close margin. This election, in fact, inaugurated an era of close presidential races. Beaten, Van Buren nevertheless remained strong as a party leader. In the Northeast and the West particularly, he and his colleagues had employed federal patronage with care in building powerful state organizations. Even in defeat, Van Buren remained a political professional in assuming the "responsibilities" of titular leadership, the first Democratic presidential nominee to do so. In Van Buren's view, the creation of a national political party was vital and honorable work:

> But knowing, as all men of sense know, that political parties are inseparable from free governments, and that in many and material respects they are highly useful to the country, I never could bring myself for my part to deprecate their existence. . . . The disposition to abuse power, so deeply planted in the human heart, can by no other means be effectively checked; and it has always struck me as more honorable and manly and more in harmony with the character of our People and of our Institutions to deal with the subject of Political Parties in a sincere and wiser spirit.[2]

Lindenwald, Van Buren's home in New York, became something of a national party headquarters as plans for assisting Democrats in various key local elections in 1841 and in the congressional elections of 1842 proceeded apace. Democratic gains in these elections were generally credited to these efforts.

A Van Buren comeback, however, was not in the cards. President Harrison's death elevated to the Presidency a states' rights Democrat devoted to the defeat of Henry Clay in the Whig Party and Martin Van Buren in the Democratic. President Tyler, an anomaly in American history books for his lack of glamour and apparent lack of distinct party affiliation, soon proved himself a match for the two major party leaders of his day, Clay and Van Buren. In accomplishing the retirement of those two men from presidential politics, Tyler had the assistance of another forgotten giant of American party politics, Senator Robert J. Walker, the "Wizard of Mississippi."

Son of a Supreme Court justice and son-in-law to the Bache-Dallas political families in Pennsylvania, Walker migrated to Mississippi in

---

[2] *Autobiography of Martin Van Buren,* ed. by John C. Fitzpatrick (Washington, D.C.: Superintendent of Documents, 1920).

1826 to practice law. Within a half-dozen years, he became leader of the Jacksonians there, Mississippi's United States senator, and spokesman for the Southwest in congressional politics. It was Walker, in alliance with Calhoun, who devised the strategy for denying Van Buren the nomination at the 1844 convention.

At issue was the question of immediate annexation of Texas. Northern Democrats were opposed to the admission of another slave state; southerners sought admission without delay. Van Buren, as titular leader speaking on the most controversial issues of his day, took the view that annexation was clearly constitutional but inexpedient in view of the possibility of war with Mexico. The statement provided a rallying point for anti-Van Buren annexationists.

A second annexationist group was led by Calhoun, who, significantly, was invited to join Tyler's Cabinet as Secretary of State just prior to the 1844 national convention. A third group consisted of border state forces led by Cave Johnson of Tennessee, who was also managing the only campaign for the vice-presidential nomination in the party's history. His candidate was Governor James K. Polk.

The Van Buren forces came to the convention in strength; fourteen state conventions, four congressional district conventions, and one state legislative caucus had instructed their delegates to support the former President for a third nomination. The committed votes came to 159, which was 18 short of the two thirds needed to nominate— that is, if the two-thirds rule (originally designed to eliminate Van Buren's opponents in 1832) were again adopted.

Senator Walker moved readoption of the rule as soon as the delegates convened. Debate raged for two days. On the roll call, Virginia, under the leadership of the Speaker of the House of Representatives, George C. Dromgoole, long a Van Buren ally, withdrew from the floor. At the end of the roll, Virginia cast its 17 votes for retention of the two-thirds rule. This was the critical margin, 148 to 118. This defeat ended Van Buren's prospects: the first nominating ballot gave him 146 votes, 31 short of the necessary two thirds.

A stalemate persisted for seven ballots. On the eighth ballot a new name, James K. Polk, was added to the roster, supported mainly by the Van Buren faction in the Massachusetts delegation. The first "dark horse" in national convention history had been found, and on the ninth ballot his nomination was the first to break a convention stalemate.

Thus, an "impossible" factional struggle had been successfully resolved. For the first time the presidential party organization had created an original synthesis, one which held promise for unanticipated harmony, strength, and success. President Tyler, without substantial chance of receiving the regular Democratic nomination, was at all times in the background during that nominating process. He observed the results with satisfaction. Having removed Van Buren, his next target was Clay, who had just received the Whig nomination. His principal strategist and field director was again Senator Walker, whose management of the Polk campaign was outstandingly successful.

The Polk Cabinet was staffed largely with men highly experienced in party operations. With a powerhouse of politicians surrounding him, President Polk made the unfortunate categorical commitment to serve only one term. Consequently, every policy decision of his Administration was fraught with implications for the succession. Wrote Polk: ". . . I am left without any certain or reliable support in Congress, and especially in the Senate. Each leader looks to his own advancement more than he does to the success of my measures." [3]

To handle the public monies in the Jackson–Van Buren tradition, the Polk Administration, under the guiding hand of Secretary Walker, restored the independent treasury. To start the tariff rate down, a Calhoun objective for years, a Walker-designed tariff law was enacted. Annexationists, North and South, were delighted by the settlement reached with the British bringing Oregon under American jurisdiction. The Oregon settlement put American boundaries at the Pacific for the first time and added a free territory. The Mexican War, aside from putting over $100 million in military spending into circulation, acquired for the United States all of the land from the Rio Grande through New Mexico to upper California.

By most political standards, the Polk Administration would be regarded as eminently successful. The acquisition of so much new territory, however, revived the issue of extension of slavery and aggravated it far beyond any degree previously known. Democrats began to call each other "Barnburners" (so antislavery as to be willing, like the Dutch farmer, to burn the barn in order to rid it of rats) and "Hunkers" (whose hunger, or "hunker," for officeholding was so intense as to compel them to cooperate with slaveholders). Those factions were particularly contentious in the 1848 national convention. In a three-way Northeast-South-Northwest contest, the conven-

---

[3] M. M. Quaife, *The Diary of James Polk* (Chicago: McClurg and Co., 1910).

tion nominated General Lewis Cass of Michigan on the fourth ballot.

Senator Jesse D. Bright of Indiana, Polk's personal representative at the convention, then moved the creation of a national committee, the first of its kind. He also directed the selection of the first Democratic national chairman, Benjamin F. Hallett of Massachusetts. The national committee was to be a permanent standing committee to serve as an organic link between conventions as well as the seat for the highest formal office in the party, the national chairmanship.

Hallett was also chairman of the platform committee whose northern majority wrote a plank on the slavery-abolition issue that was conciliatory to the South. Thus, ten years after Democrats under Van Buren had straddled the issue of abolishing slavery in the District of Columbia, the party's leaders were still trying to solve that problem by an exercise in language. But it could never be. The environment was creating new conditions and pressures.

Decade of Stalemate

Thus began a critical decade which, as the Whig Party disintegrated, found the Union's future resting heavily in the hands of the Democrats. It became an era in which the Democratic presidential candidates were "northerners with southern principles." The Democrats who became President—Pierce and Buchanan—were so cross-pressured by sectionalism that their administrations are invariably recorded in the history books as models of inertia or inept political straddling. Their lack of motion and decision reflected the stalemates of a dividing nation, unwilling or unable to go one way or another.

Northerners and southerners alike were rushing to settle the West, and with them went a fundamental economic issue: should the economy of the new territories and states be constructed upon a foundation of slave or free labor? Hanging heavily upon this issue was the future influence of the Democratic South upon the Presidency and in Congress where, proportionately speaking, the South was becoming a permanent minority.

The 1848 presidential nominee, Senator Lewis Cass, and National Chairman Hallett were Hunkers—that is, conciliatory to the southern positions on the slavery issue. Both men, together with King of Alabama, Douglas of Illinois, Buchanan of Pennsylvania, and Woodbury of New Hampshire, did their utmost to keep the party in Congress and elsewhere on a middle course. This was no easy matter. The abolitionists and the free-soil wing were being led by such experienced politicians as former President Van Buren and his son John. At the other extreme were the states' rights group led by Hunter and Mason of Virginia, Jefferson Davis, and others. Van Buren, still a power in New York, felt that the issue could no longer be postponed. He led a substantial following into the new Free Soil Party, whose presidential nomination he accepted. The defection cost the Democrats the election and the presidential wing its influence during the next three or four decades.

Most of the politicial action during the 1850's took place in Congress. Much of the strife was precipitated by the territorial gains of the Mexican War and the discovery of gold in California. Talk of secession had already begun among southern Whigs and southern Democrats in states from South Carolina to Mississippi. California was asking for admission as a free state, New Mexico was ready for territorial government, abolitionists were again demanding the end of the slave trade in the District of Columbia, and southern slaveholders were insisting upon a more severe fugitive-slave law. Debate in Congress occupied the attention of the nation for most of 1850. Once again the question of the nature of the Union brought forth the best efforts of the political giants of that day: Calhoun, Clay, Webster, Benton, Cass, young Stephen A. Douglas, William H. Seward, and others. Clay and Douglas were the major architects of a new compromise.

In the midst of it all, President Taylor died, putting Millard Fillmore, a Whig of narrow judgment and nativist tendencies, into power. Whig factions became so extreme on the Clay compromise proposals that it required the best efforts of a leading Democrat, Senator Douglas, to carry the Compromise of 1850 through Congress. California came into the Union as a free state; slave trade was prohibited in the District of Columbia; the fugitive slave laws were to be more strictly enforced, to mention only the major provisions. As in most political transactions in which all participants are powerful and hard bargainers, none of the parties was long satisfied with the deal.

The Whigs never survived the strain of the slavery issue, a grave warning to the equally torn Democrats. In many localities Democratic organizations were disintegrating or drifting into a movement calling for a new "Union Party" willing to defend the Compromise of 1850. Harassed presidential Democrats looked around for a truly "national" candidate for 1852.

A three-way deadlock among Cass, Buchanan, and Douglas developed and lasted for thirty-four ballots at the national convention.

Among Buchanan's supporters were leading southerners. Stephen A. Douglas spoke for the Northwest.

In the dark-horse tradition, a new name—General Franklin Pierce of Mexican War fame—was added and nominated on the forty-ninth ballot, retiring Cass and postponing the aspirations of Buchanan and Douglas for future years.

The Pierce Administration was almost totally immobilized by the near-equal pressures of northern and southern Democrats. The impulse of every Democratic politician was to retreat from the issue of slavery. In this spirit, Senator Douglas introduced a bill into Congress authorizing the organization of the Nebraska territory, without making reference to slavery. Before the bill became an act, however, it had been converted into an authorization for *two* territories (Kansas and Nebraska), each to decide according to the principle of *squatter sovereignty*—that is, local option—whether it would be free or slave.

Northern Democrats, northern Whigs, northern "Know-Nothings," and the Free Soil Party were outraged by the Kansas-Nebraska Act. They promptly promoted mass migrations of settlers from the East intended to save at least Kansas from slavery. Southerners started a countermigration. Civil war raged in the territory. "Bleeding Kansas" put President Pierce and Senator Douglas out of the running for 1856.

Another three-way battle developed at the 1856 national convention. John Slidell led the Buchanan forces with great skill, defeating a Pierce-Douglas alliance on a test vote. On the sixteenth ballot, Buchanan had 168 and Douglas 122 votes, with Buchanan still short of the necessary two thirds. At this point, Douglas, twenty-two years Buchanan's junior, withdrew his name. Slidell's victory was capped by the addition of a young southerner, John C. Breckinridge, to the ticket.

Buchanan was elected with only five of the sixteen "free" states supporting him; fourteen of the fifteen "slave" states, on the other hand, gave him their electoral votes. Having asserted such influence at the 1856 convention, little wonder that Slidell and other southerners, aided and abetted by a friendly President, were in 1860 so unwilling to concede party leadership to Douglas.

Defection, Defeat, and Disaster

Senator Slidell was a dominant influence in the Buchanan Administration. The southern view was further reinforced by the Dred

Scott decision, in which the most extreme southern position on slave property was endorsed by the Supreme Court.

President Buchanan, anticipating the admission of Kansas under extremely difficult conditions, appointed the politically seasoned Robert J. Walker as its governor. Through a ruse that was roundly denounced by Free Soilers, a draft constitution was written at Lecompton, Kansas, which protected slave property already in that territory. Buchanan and Walker urged upon Congress the admission of Kansas under this constitution, but were overridden by the House. During this debate, Douglas broke with Buchanan, thereby establishing himself as the leader of the antislavery wing of the party.

The pace and intensity of the struggle over the slavery issue reached grim proportions by 1858. Slidell tried to read Douglas out of the party, urging the Administration to withdraw patronage from Douglas supporters in Illinois. Despite the pressure, in his famous debates with Abraham Lincoln, Douglas asserted his "Freeport Doctrine," denying that Congress had power to force slavery upon a territory against the will of its people.

Meanwhile, the Republican Party was emerging from the shambles left by the Whigs and was adopting a hard antislavery position. Both houses, meeting in Thirty-sixth Congress (1859–1860), were scenes of tumult. Debaters engaged in personal invective. The galleries participated loudly in the excitement on the floor. Observers speculated how many and which of the members were armed. On the eve of the Democratic national convention of 1860, the embittered and the extremists were among the loudest voices to be heard.

The Slidell-Douglas feud continued right into the national conventions of 1860. The margins of factional victory in the Charleston convention were narrow and costly. A one-vote margin in the national committee put a Douglas man into the temporary chairmanship, but an anti-Douglas man won the permanent chairmanship. The Douglas forces won a modification of the unit rule in delegation balloting, but Slidell's proposal for completing the platform before the nomination carried in another debate.

Out of the southern-dominated platform committee came a majority report promising congressional protection of slave property. The Douglas men wrote the principal minority report reiterating the squatter sovereignty position. An alliance between the Buchanan forces and the southern ultras sent both reports back to committee, 152 to 151.

The platform committee again worked on the language of the platform. With greater candor than ever, it drafted a statement ac knowledging publicly that a difference of opinion existed within th party with respect to slavery. On the floor of the convention, thi revision of what had been the Douglas minority report carried, 165- 138. The Douglas manager rose to make a peace offer, but a souther walkout had already begun, Alabama in the lead. The seceders in cluded most of the Mississippi, Louisiana, South Carolina, Florida and Texas delegations, who immediately organized their own Con stitutional Democratic national convention.

Chairman Cushing soon after ruled that the two thirds needed to nominate would have to be based upon the 303 votes originally sen to the convention rather than upon the 252 delegates who remained after the walkout. After fifty-seven ballots, Douglas was still shor of the necessary 202. The weary convention adjourned, to meet in Baltimore six weeks later.

During those weeks a great struggle for moral and numerical ad vantage took place in Congress. Jefferson Davis repeated the deman of the southern ultras for a "Congressional Slave Code." Douglas replied that only a majority at the national convention and not a minority in the Senate could properly prescribe what would be the test of party loyalty.

At Baltimore the big test came on the credentials committee report. The Douglas men were ready to readmit all of the bolters except those from former Vice-President King's Alabama and Slidell's Louisiana. This was upheld in a 199-150 floor vote. Now the Virginia delegation led the departing Democrats, who included the delegates from North Carolina, Tennessee, California, Oregon, most of Mary- land, most of Kentucky, Missouri, and Arkansas. With them went Permanent Chairman Cushing.

The "Seceders" convention, with Cushing in the chair, composed itself of some 230 delegates, of whom 115 had been from the au- thentic membership of the original convention. Of these, approx- imately 58 were Buchanan appointees. Breckinridge became the nominee of the southern Democrats. In the regular convention, Douglas prevailed.

In the southern view, the Breckinridge candidacy was launched from a position of great strength. He was, after all, the incumbent Vice-President, with the support of the President and the largest number of normally Democratic states. Douglas, on the other hand, had to face the new Republican Party in the Northeast and the Mid- west.

From the Douglas point of view, two decades of compromise on the slavery issue had given the southerners a disproportionate influence in the presidential party. If the southerners would not accept Douglas, to whom they would have access in the Presidency, they might get an antislavery Republican like Lincoln, to whom they did not have access. Miscalculation followed misperception. Although moderates on both sides spent most of the campaign months trying to negotiate reconciliation or combined electoral slates, the extremists prevailed.

Lincoln's election brought talk of secession. Head of a repudiated party, President Buchanan did little to restrain his southern colleagues. As a President-elect without official power, Lincoln, in the four months between election and inauguration, could do nothing to head off catastrophe. The situation was ideal for extremist maneuvers, and these took place soon enough at Fort Sumter.

CHAPTER 5

Renaissance of the Presidential Wing

THE SUBSTANCE and vitality that Jackson and Van Buren gave to the office of President and to the presidential wing of the Democratic Party were sustained by Polk but dissipated by Pierce and Buchanan. As the out-party during the Civil War and Reconstruction periods, Democrats were in no position to employ the resources of the Presidency for the reconstruction of the presidential party. The great achievement of Tilden, whose political career and contributions to the party have largely gone unrecognized, was to gather the party's own resources sufficiently for near-victories in 1876 and 1880 and for the return to power under Cleveland in 1884.

The presidential party under Cleveland matched the Republicans vote for vote and policy for policy—leading to the charge that the major parties were as alike as Tweedledee and Tweedledum—in one of the most closely contested electoral periods in American history. Then, with Bryan as titular leader, the presidential wing became something of a political megaphone for the populist and progressive movements of the decades between 1890 and 1920. Wilson's experiment with parliament-style leadership failed, but his assertions of the party responsibilities of Presidents started the Presidency and the presidential party well along the road back to the relative influence it enjoyed in the Jacksonian era. In keeping with the decade-long strides of party history, Wilson built the presidential party that paved the way for Roosevelt's New Deal.

However, before the renaissance came the fall. With the departure of the South from the Union in 1861, the Democratic Party was deprived of some 100 Electoral College votes. If the party had any future at all, it rested within three clusters of competitive two-party states: New York and New Jersey in the East; Ohio, Illinois, and Indiana in the Midwest; California and Oregon in the West. The biggest were New York (35 votes) and Ohio (23 votes). And these two states became the poles of a wartime factionalism within the party.

War Democrats and Peace Democrats

The passing of Stephen A. Douglas in 1861 left the Democrats leaderless and on the point of following the Whig Party into limbo. Fully half of the party's popular vote had been in the southern states, and these had departed. The western and eastern wings had been held together by Douglas of Illinois and National Chairman August Belmont of New York. With Douglas gone, almost complete leadership devolved upon Belmont, who promptly placed the "War Democrats" behind Lincoln's efforts to preserve the Union. Meanwhile, "Peace Democrats"—former Breckinridge and Bell supporters philosophically bound to the states' rights position—began to gather around Clement L. Vallandigham of Ohio and Mayor Fernando Wood of New York. Factional struggles continued, but without the southern brethren.

A member of the House of Representatives and an active manager of the Douglas presidential campaign, Vallandigham saw himself as the successor to the mantle of the deceased "Little Giant." In Congress he devoted much time to the search for a compromise in the sectional conflict, his neo-Calhounian plan premised upon a division of the country into four sections. The Vallandigham plans never caught on, for they represented a locking of the barn after the horses were gone. As his personal leadership failed to take hold, Vallandigham led the Peace Democrats of the Northwest toward increasingly severe criticism of the conduct of the war, opposition to conscription, and endless reiteration of proposals for a negotiated peace in which the Northwest might play a major role as negotiator.

By 1863 many of the more extreme Peace Democrats were resorting to secret organization in an effort to supplement or replace the regular party machinery. These clandestine societies maintained military subsidiaries. The War Democrats of the Northwest reacted with the establishment of "Loyal Leagues." Republicans enjoyed the Democratic factional difficulties and bestowed the label "Copperhead" upon the Peace Democrats.

The Peace Democrats were not alone in their efforts to bring about a negotiated peace. The British and the French, with substantial economic interest in both the North and South, maintained various types of pressure in order to end the devastation of the Civil War. At the head of the War Democrats, National Chairman Belmont offered President Lincoln specific proposals for a negotiated peace, recommending general amnesty for political offenses, a national constitutional convention to reconstruct the federal compact, and review of the constitutionality of slave property-holding. Belmont proposed federal assumption of both northern and southern war debts, a plan similar to Lincoln's, in which all Americans would participate in rebuilding the southern battlegrounds.

Belmont also suggested the maintenance of a large standing army and navy after the cessation of hostilities, recognition of a much overlooked military fact relevant to events leading up to the Civil War. At the time of the attack upon Fort Sumter, fully nine tenths of the Federal Army was in the Midwest and on the frontiers of the Far West; only about a thousand troops were stationed around the District of Columbia, an easy prey. In the East, only the New York and Massachusetts state militias on the one side and the Virginia and Louisiana state militias on the other could be considered equipped and manned for combat. In a word, southern ultras pressing for military action in 1860–1861 had substantial grounds for thinking they had a better-than-even chance of winning. What the ultras did not fully anticipate was the North's willingness to pay a high price for the preservation of the Union.

By 1864 most Democratic presidential timber had run into trouble. Vallandigham had been defeated for reelection to Congress and for election as governor of Ohio. In New York, Governor Horatio Seymour found himself confronted by draft riots and accused of softness toward the war effort. More extreme War Democrats were trying to create a "Union" Party that could support Lincoln, and National Chairman Belmont was warning regular Democrats away from the new organization. In their search for a nominee, Democrats finally turned to General George B. McClellan, who had become a popular martyr at the hands of the Radical Republicans.

Recalling that in 1860 he had been a minority President, Lincoln adopted in 1864 the strategy of creating a "Union" Party, with a War Democrat from a border state on his ticket. As military governor of Tennessee and a well-known War Democrat, Andrew Johnson met the specifications and accepted the nomination.

A glance at the following table indicates that, even without southern Democrats, the party was hardly a pushover in the presidential contests from 1864 to 1872. The closeness of the disputed Hayes-Tilden election of 1876 and the tight race of 1880 gave particular impetus to the Radical Republican strategy for keeping the southern states from rejoining the Union as long as possible.

Per Cent Popular Vote for President

Year	Democratic	Republican
1864	44.8%	55.2%
1868	47.3	52.7
1872	43.8	55.6
1876	50.9	47.9
1880	48.2	48.3

Most decisive for the 1864 election, however, were the victories being turned in just prior to Election Day by General Ulysses S. Grant. President Lincoln was reelected, and General McClellan went on a tour of Europe.

The end of the war brought no end to extremism. The Radical Republicans demanded a vindictive peace. Confusion continued in both presidential and congressional politics, where one could find Conservative Republicans, Administration Republicans, Radical Republicans, Unionists, War Democrats, and Peace Democrats.

Lincoln's assassination put Johnson in as anomalous a political position as John Tyler had experienced in 1841. The Democratic press, both North and South, after brief expressions of doubt, began to hail Johnson as their own. Johnson's expressions of determination to carry on Lincoln's Reconstruction program made it clear to the Radicals that Johnson was not of their fraternity. Would President Johnson align himself as a Democrat, a Unionist, or a Republican?

Only the Radical Republican leadership in Congress was clear in its objectives. Lincoln's plan for southern Reconstruction was cast aside by them and the Radical plan adopted in its place. With the Vice-Presidency vacant and a Radical, Ben Wade, holding the presidency of the Senate, next in line of presidential succession, the Radicals embarked upon an audacious attempt to remove President Johnson by impeachment for violation of the Tenure of Office Act.

In December, 1867, Secretary of War Stanton, a Radical sympathizer, provoked a dispute with Johnson and was subsequently removed without the required "advice and consent" of the Senate. Johnson named General Grant as Stanton's successor. Radicals in the Senate, with thirty-six votes needed to impeach, gathered only thirty-five. A single vote kept the Presidency out of Radical hands, but only temporarily. General Grant, now a national hero, received the Republican nomination in 1868 from a convention dominated by the Radicals.

Frustration marked the efforts of Democratic presidential politicians at every turn. McClellan, hardly cut out for practical politics, had gone abroad and stayed there. President Johnson never clearly grasped the party helm. Vallandigham and George Pendleton were locked in a bitter feud for control of the Ohio Democratic organization. Seymour, over the protests of New York State Chairman Samuel J. Tilden, took himself firmly out of the race. Robert J. Walker wrote Tilden a careful analysis on the availability of Winfield Scott Hancock, a politically inexperienced but popular Union general. Others proposed Senator Thomas A. Hendricks, a "sound money" mid-westerner; the question of currency soundness and credit conditions had come into prominence with postwar inflation and agricultural depression.

After twenty-two ballots, Hancock and Hendricks were obviously stalemated, and a compromise was sought. A Pendleton-Vallandigham truce in the Ohio delegation gave that state's vote, in a surprise maneuver, to Seymour. New York followed suit. Seymour became the reluctant "hard money" nominee, for whom the convention wrote a greenback platform. The ensuing campaign was equally reluctant and divided.

Tilden and Out-Party Revival

What did emerge from the 1868 campaign was a new figure in presidential politics, Samuel J. Tilden. A corporation lawyer who had accumulated substantial wealth, Tilden had been active in New York politics since the 1830's. He was a careful observer of such professionals as Van Buren and a series of Tammany leaders. In time, he became a political associate of Horatio Seymour, working with and against Tammany as the situation demanded.

Cultured, aloof, and incessantly in poor health, Tilden never quite achieved a large popular following. He was a party organizer and a politician's politician. As Seymour's campaign manager in 1868, Tilden supplemented the lethargic and divided official party machinery with a vigorous new organization called "The Order of the Union Democracy." Like Van Buren before him, Tilden's figure would be seen across Democratic presidential politics for two decades. Unlike Van Buren, however, Tilden never reached the Presidency.

His Cabinet crowded with personal friends as ill-experienced in politics as he himself, President Grant soon found himself surrounded by the Radical Republicans and their Senate "Stalwart Cabal" as he had never been on the battlefield. The Radicals kept a tight hand on the distribution of the patronage, on the maintenance of a high tariff, and the administration of the Reconstruction program for the South. From New England and the Midwest, Republican liberals like Charles Sumner and Carl Schurz enjoyed little access to their President and had less fortune with the advancement of their program for civil service reform and a liberal southern policy. By 1871 Horace Greeley, publisher of the *Tribune* and long active in New York Republican politics, joined a factional bolt that grew to become the Liberal Republican Party.

For the leaderless Democrats, still incapacitated by the absence of their southern wing and facing a second-term campaign against a popular incumbent, a gnawing dilemma presented itself: Could an alliance with the new Liberal Republican Party produce a victory? Could the Liberal Republicans later be absorbed into the Democratic rank-and-file? Would the combined reformist elements in the Democratic and the new party make possible a potent attack upon the corruption becoming visible in the Grant Administration?

The Liberal Republicans met in 1872 to make up their national ticket. As they watched the proceedings from afar, Democrats generally expected Supreme Court Justice David Davis, Lincoln's political associate of many years, or Charles Francis Adams to be the nominee; either man would have been acceptable to a majority of the Democratic leadership. Instead, after a rugged factional fight, the Liberals came up with Horace Greeley! Having already paved the way for an endorsement, the Democratic leadership could hardly turn back, despite strong opposition to the endorsement plan from the New York, New Jersey, Pennsylvania, and Delaware organizations.

Tilden's political associate, Augustus Schell, took on the management of the ill-fated Greeley campaign and did much with the opportunity to strengthen ties with the reemerging Democratic leadership in the South.

The election of 1872 was disastrous for the Democrats if votes only are taken into account. Otherwise, the campaign brought a substantial part of the South back into active participation in presidential politics, recruited large numbers of Republican liberals into the Democratic fold, elevated the reform issue to top place in national politics, and put the Tilden forces in control of the presidential party machinery. Tilden, as governor of New York in 1874 and destroyer of the New York Canal Ring in 1875, became the unchallenged front-runner for the presidential nomination in 1876. He received the nomination on the second ballot. There was midwestern dissatisfaction with his hard-money views and opposition from Tammany leaders, but the issue that united all factions was reform.

Less than a dozen years had passed since the termination of Civil War hostilities, but the South continued to be more torn by Reconstruction than it had been by cannon and shell. The southern political scene was a kaleidoscope of carpetbaggers, scalawags, the Ku Klux Klan, anti-Republican "rifle clubs," strikes, riots, and massacres. The southern ballot box floated in blood and strife, particularly in Louisiana, South Carolina, and Florida.

These, in fact, were the states whose election returns in the Tilden-Hayes contest were subject to question. Two sets of returns were produced in each state. Tilden received, nationally, approximately 250,000 more popular votes than Hayes, but neither party could be certain of more than 165 electoral votes. Twenty votes—those of Louisiana, South Carolina, Florida, plus one from Oregon—arrived late, of questionable validity and contested.

From election day to inauguration, the two parties, through press and local organizations, conducted themselves as hostile armies. President Grant insisted upon a nonmilitary solution to be worked out in Congress. Both Tilden and Hayes acted with exceptional moderation. The Democratic caucus organized a permanent advisory committee of eleven representatives and six senators to devote full attention to the problem. Congress established a special Electoral Commission to determine which sets of returns would be accepted. Not until March 2 was the outcome known, and this outcome was the result of a one-vote majority in the Electoral Commission. Hayes was elected.

Disappointment led to recrimination among fellow Democrats. Over sixty, afflicted with arthritis and other ailments, Tilden went into semiretirement. His associates, however, kept alive his image as a victim of fraud at the hands of his enemies and stupidity among his friends. Thus it appeared—until the *New York Tribune* released a series of telegrams sent between Tilden's nephew and a Tilden manager indicating that there had been bribery negotiations aimed at purchasing votes for Tilden. A congressional committee investigated and confirmed the story. The developments destroyed Tilden's political future, despite his personal innocence. Overnight, forty years of Tilden's devotion to reform were obliterated by the brush of scandal.

Tilden was uncertain how to proceed in 1880. On the one hand, he wrote a letter to the New York delegation requesting an "honorable discharge." On the other hand, he told his friend and aide, Daniel Manning, that he would not accept a nomination unless it were unanimous. Taken at his word, his name was not put in nomination. A four-way race among Hancock, Bayard, Payne, and Thurman emerged.

On the second ballot, with a push from the Tilden forces, Hancock received the nomination. Tilden men retained control of the party machinery and the presidential campaign organization. Despite a poorly financed and generally inept campaign, Hancock came within several thousand votes of a popular majority.

Hancock retired. Tilden remained the principal elder in the Democratic clan. His influence continued to be felt through his younger associates: New York State Chairman Manning and Colonel Daniel Lamont. This influence was particularly noticed in the New York organization as it prepared to chose its 1882 gubernatorial candidate. Tilden's choice was the reform mayor of Buffalo, Grover Cleveland.

Cleveland won the governorship and, in the short space of two years, became Tilden's heir to the presidential party mantle, winning the 1884 nomination in two ballots. Cleveland's election, in another close outcome, capped nearly two decades of Tilden's influence in Democratic politics.

Cleveland's Recapture of the Presidency

The Cleveland victory marked the return of the Democrats to control of the White House after twenty-four years. It was a mixed blessing. So great had the presidential job patronage become and so overflowing the federal treasury that the problems of affluence became the major preoccupations of the new President.

In postmasterships alone, there were more than fifty thousand appointments to be handled, and tens of thousands of other federal jobs were also to be distributed. Every presidential appointment produced at least one disappointed Democratic applicant and several offended Democratic civil service reformers. The patronage issue remained a difficult one for several Presidents.

Although the South continued to struggle under the burden of Reconstruction costs and the farmer rarely saw the cheap money he so ardently advocated, national industrial growth and foreign trade had produced excise and tariff revenue sufficient to put the aforementioned large surplus into the treasury. Currency and tariff policy became the most compelling public issues of the Cleveland era. Should the treasury pay out millions in gold bullion in order to purchase the fixed amount of silver for coinage required by the Bland-Allison Act? Cleveland favored dropping silver coinage in order to protect the government's gold stocks. Within a decade this position isolated him from the mainstream of the party.

Somewhat Jacksonian in style and content was Cleveland's tariff message of December, 1887. Tariff revision was *the* chosen issue of that message. A high tariff not only protected "the interests," he argued, but also made the federal treasury a grab bag for the greedy. Reduction of rates was essential. The Republican titular leader, James G. Blaine, took the occasion to reaffirm that party's protectionist position. Protectionists within the Democratic Party, somewhat less vocally, took to their ramparts; the issue became a factional touchstone.

Cleveland, in 1888, received a hundred-thousand-vote popular plurality, but these votes turned up in the wrong places. New York went Republican by only thirteen thousand votes, and its Electoral College votes put Harrison into the White House. In an era when local registration safeguards were almost nonexistent, the Republican national committee was able to mobilize three important "movements" of voters from Pennsylvania to New York City. It is estimated that some fifty thousand "floaters" were contracted for, although a much smaller number were delivered to the New York City precincts.

Cleveland retired to the practice of law in New York and maintained relative silence on public policy and his availability for renomination. The issue upon which Cleveland eventually chose to take a strong public stand as a private citizen was hardly calculated to bring fellow Democrats in certain sections of the country running to his support. The potent silver interests in the Mountain States and the aggrieved agricultural interests in the South and Midwest were insisting upon the maintenance of a bimetallic currency, the former to dispose of the growing supply of silver and the latter to make currency and credit more readily available. The depressed agricultural economy brought in a vigorous populism and, along with it, a Democratic sweep in the congressional elections of 1890. The party seemed on the verge of being overtaken by the silverite forces, and the former President, early in 1891, put his future on the line by declaring unqualifiedly that free coinage of silver was a "dangerous and reckless experiment." The newspapers of the South and the West were unrestrained in their condemnation of him.

Opposition to Cleveland gathered momentum in other corners of the party. Protectionists such as Senator Arthur Pue Gorman of Maryland were active. In New York, Governor David B. Hill carried on an old feud with the ex-President. Even National Chairman Calvin Brice expressed doubt that Cleveland could muster the necessary two thirds for renomination. The genius of the Cleveland renomination campaign was William C. Whitney, the wealthy corporation lawyer who had served as a political adjutant of both Tilden and Cleveland over the years. It was Whitney's quiet leadership that overcame every obstacle at the 1892 convention.

Once again the popular vote was evenly divided, but this time well over a million votes went to the Populist nominee. Through their numerous local alliances with Democrats, the Populist leadership found itself in a substantial bargaining position to influence Democratic Party decisions in the next elections. Events aided their cause.

As Cleveland awaited his second inauguration, the economic horizons filled with signs of impending collapse. Financial and congressional leaders spoke with unprecedented urgency about the need to repeal the Sherman Silver Purchase Act, upon which they placed blame for the precarious conditions of the gold supply, credit, and price structure. By May, the Panic of 1893 was upon the nation.

Congress convened in special session, at the President's call, in August and fought over the repeal issue until November. From the southerners and the westerners came charges that the President was "the tool of Wall Street." Great oratory was produced, and among the greatest was that of a young congressman from Nebraska, William Jennings Bryan.

Cleveland's second Administration was a troubled one. The depression aggravated the party's differences of view on currency as never before. Labor unrest led to such crises as the Pullman strike in Chicago in 1894, a strike broken by Cleveland's dispatch of federal troops. The protectionists in both parties undid the Administration's reductionist bills on tariff rates. And younger leaders such as Ben Tillman and Champ Clark fired steady criticism at Cleveland. The midterm election gave the Republicans and the Populists such impressive margins that the President's prestige in the party never recovered.

Bryan's Silver Coins and Crosses of Gold

In both parties the free-silver organizers were on the move. Silver Democrats launched the American Bimetallic League. Silver Republicans promoted the National Bimetallic Union. Both merged into the American Bimetallic Union. In July, 1895, a conference of "bimetallic" Democrats, intent upon capturing the next national convention, met in Washington and organized the Bimetallic Democratic National Committee.

As the silverites mobilized, President Cleveland remained silent about his own renomination intentions, thus keeping his sound-money supporters off balance. Whitney based his 1896 convention strategy on the expectation that he would have one third of the votes, enough to veto a free-silver nomination; he was profoundly surprised to find himself short at convention time.

The national convention consisted of 930 votes, of which 312 were needed for a veto on the nomination. A test vote over the temporary chairmanship revealed the majority held by the silverites: 556 to 349. There was little doubt that a free-silver leader would be nominated. The question was: "Which one?"

The strongest contenders were Richard P. Bland and Horace Boies. A well-known name in the silver cause, but one rarely mentioned as presidential timber, was thirty-six-year-old William Jennings Bryan. However, several unusual factors were working in Bryan's favor. The Bland and Boies candidacies were about to stalemate each other. The silver leaders could ill afford a drawn-out contest, as their collective strength lay so close to the two-thirds majority. Of all the silver candidates, only Bryan was popular in such pro-silver splinter parties as the Populists, the Silver Republicans, and the National Silver Party. Finally, a substantial number of southern delegates had become committed to Bryan as their second choice. In this setting, Senator Jones, chairman of the platform committee, invited Bryan to sum up the arguments of the silver side in the floor debate. With a keenness of judgment about the national convention process that enabled him to influence its decisions for nearly two decades, Bryan carefully prepared his presentation. In fact, during the evening before, he told a delegation from the Silver Republican Party that he expected to be the nominee.

The following day, as he spoke probably the most-quoted oration of national convention history, the marginal votes were already shifting in his direction. Said the "Boy Orator": "We shall answer their demands for a gold standard by saying to them, you shall not press down upon the brow of labor this crown of thorns. You shall not crucify mankind upon a cross of gold." On the fifth ballot, the prize was his.

But not the Presidency. Governor William McKinley and his multi-millionaire campaign manager, Mark Hanna, were formidable enough opponents. But once again some of the main elements of defeat lay in the Democratic Party itself. President Cleveland sat out the campaign. A substantial number of his political colleagues either quietly supported the McKinley candidacy or gave their energies to the new "Gold Democratic Party." Probably the most difficult aspect of this campaign, however, was the necessity to coordinate the efforts of *four* political parties: Democrats, Populists, National Silverites, and Silver Republicans. The difficulties of coordination left little more than October to carry on the campaign among the voters.

The McKinley Administration rode upon an era of prosperity, national self-confidence, and expansionist fervor. The land-space between the Atlantic and the Pacific was filled; only Arizona, New Mexico, and Oklahoma remained to be admitted to the Union. American free-lancers were prospecting in Alaska, upsetting a monarchy in Hawaii, selling supplies to Cuban revolutionaries, filibustering up and down Central America, investing in South American enterprises, discussing an interoceanic canal across Nicaragua, and reaching advanced stages of monopolistic industrial enterprise at home. Gold discoveries in the Klondike, for all practical purposes, solved the bimetallic currency problem.

War with Spain seemed almost a sideshow, leading to independence for Cuba, acquisition of Puerto Rico and Guam, and, for $20 million, the purchase of the Philippines. A continent-wide nation with overseas possessions and investments, the American people were now world politicians, although for three or four more decades many would resist the thought and the action.

Bryan made of himself a full-time titular leader, writing an account of the 1896 campaign as merely *The First Battle,* and between 1897 and 1899 traveling some ninety-three thousand miles on the lecture circuit. His principal subjects were money, trusts, and imperialism. On the organizational side, Bryan encouraged the development of local clubs and their parent organization, The National Association of Democratic Clubs. In 1900, William Randolph Hearst became its president.

Across the nation, Democratic alliances with the Populists and the Silver Republicans became unsettled. The conditions under which Gold Democrats might return were not easily formulated at the convention of 1900. Even Bryan's inevitable renomination seemed to be a kind of postponement; David B. Hill, now senator from New York, made it clear that the demands of the eastern wing would grow louder. Selection of the temporary chairman, various platform planks, and other convention decisions were decided in close votes. Selection of a vice-presidential nominee became an awkward hassle among Democrats, Populists, and Silver Republicans in the lobbies. Former Vice-President Adlai E. Stevenson was settled upon as a compromise.

The Bryan Interregnum

The election of 1900 revealed the same one-party character of the electorate that had emerged four years earlier. Some fifteen states, mostly in the South, were safely Democratic; another fifteen were as surely Republican. Roughly one third of the Electoral College, found in approximately ten states, was contestable. That contest was lost to President McKinley as the nation enjoyed its incomparable prosperity.

Bryan retired to the publication of a weekly newspaper called *The Commoner,* wrote *The Second Battle,* lectured interminably, and commented, with increasing religious allusion, upon the great issues of the day. His reformism, for want of party rostrum, was expressed through *The Commoner,* where he favored such "radical" (for that day) innovations as a federal income tax, direct election of United States senators, prohibition of the sale of intoxicating beverages, women's suffrage, a department of labor in the Cabinet, publicity of election campaign expenditures, and independence for the Philippines.

A turnabout in presidential politics came with the assassination of President McKinley. Theodore Roosevelt's brand of progressivism shifted the stance of the Republican Party noticeably closer to Bryan's. The new President even launched an antimonopoly crusade.

In the Democratic Party, William Randolph Hearst, fiercely antitrust and prolabor, prepared to bid for the Bryan supporters at the next national convention. He had Bryan's endorsement. As Hearst set out on the delegate-collecting trail, he encountered a tough coalition of state and local bosses typical of the era: Roger Sullivan in Illinois, David B. Hill and Tammany's Murphy in New York, Tom

Taggart of Indiana, Gorman of Maryland, and others. With no notable candidate of their own, the anti-Bryan forces, at first stalking behind the name of former President Cleveland, eventually settled upon Judge Alton B. Parker, a distinguished but little known New York jurist.

At the convention Bryan led and lost the fight to seat the Hearst delegation from Illinois, 647–299. He was somewhat more successful in the platform committee where an anti-bimetallism plank was set aside for silence on the issue.

When the nominations—his own name not among them—had been completed, Bryan took the rostrum to say: "Eight years ago a Democratic national convention placed in my hand the standard of the party and commissioned me as its candidate. Four years later that commission was renewed. I come tonight to this Democratic convention to return the commission." Titular leadership, even in defeat, was for Bryan an active responsibility. He mentioned several men for whom the entire party could unite, Parker's name *not* among them. But Parker had it on the first ballot.

The anti-Bryan leaders, flushed with victory, seemed intent upon destroying the Bryan influence forever. Although Bryan had won the fight in the platform committee, the entire currency issue was reopened by a telegram from Parker asserting his unequivocal support of the gold standard and asking that his nomination be withdrawn if this proved unsatisfactory to the majority. The unprecedented tactic threw the convention into turmoil. The delegates replied with the statement that the monetary issue was not "a possible issue in this campaign."

But the last word was Bryan's. Bryan came into the Parker campaign in mid-July willing, he wrote in *The Commoner,* to support the nominee because of the party's anti-imperialism stand, its program to reduce the standing army, Roosevelt's position on the race issue, and Roosevelt's warlike foreign policy. On the other hand, Bryan wrote, Parker was clearly on the wrong side of the money, antitrust, and labor issues. Then, without explicitly stating the assumption that Parker would be defeated, Bryan concluded: "As soon as the election is over, I shall . . . undertake to organize for the campaign of 1908. . . . I shall start out to reorganize the Democratic Party along radical lines." [1]

The election retired Parker and Hill. With Hearst the only alterna-

[1] *The New York Times,* July 22, 1904.

tive to Bryan, local leaders began to fall in line behind Bryan for the 1908 nomination. Nominated on the first ballot, Bryan faced President Roosevelt's hand-picked successor, William Howard Taft. The Presidency itself became headquarters for Taft's campaign management. Hearst, thoroughly disappointed by the Democratic Party's failure to give him its nomination, started a third party aimed at Bryan's defeat.

Despite his third defeat, the stubborn Bryan would not let go. But important and skillful challengers were appearing. Champ Clark of Missouri became Speaker of the House of Representatives in 1911 when a Democratic majority took control. A respected southerner, Oscar Underwood of Alabama, was another presidential prospect with roots in the House. Governor Judson Harmon of Ohio had substantial support in the Northeast. Woodrow Wilson, a former president of Princeton University, elected governor of New Jersey in 1910, was a fourth prospect. Bryan enjoyed the multifaceted race, doing all that he could to broadcast the impression that he, Bryan, was the only alternative in a stalemate between Clark and Wilson.

When Bryan declined a national committee offer that he serve as temporary chairman and keynote speaker at the 1912 convention, the committee turned to Alton B. Parker, the second senior man in the party. Bryan used this selection as an issue upon which to test who were the conservatives and who the progressives. He nominated his 1908 runningmate, John W. Kern of Indiana, as an alternative to Parker. Kern took the podium to decline, appealed to the New York leaders to accept some compromise, but received no response. Whereupon Kern nominated Bryan for the temporary chairmanship. Parker won the chair, 579–508, with the support of Underwood and Harmon votes. Wilson votes went to Bryan. The Clark following was evenly divided. Over a hundred thousand telegrams descended upon the convention decrying the conservative tactics. Bryan was to be in the saddle for a while longer.

His next maneuver was to isolate the New York leaders. Bryan introduced a resolution asking the convention to declare itself "opposed to the nomination of any candidate for President who is the representative of or under obligation to J. Pierpont Morgan, Thomas F. Ryan, August Belmont, or any other member of the privilege-hunting and favor-seeking class." A second section of this resolution demanded the "withdrawal from this convention of any delegate or delegates" representing these interests.

Delegates "screeched," "frothed at the mouth," and one even proposed the assassination of Bryan. During the debate Bryan withdrew the second section, leaving the first section to be passed by an overwhelming majority. Any nominee now obviously had to win the endorsement of *both* Bryan and the New York leaders.

Choosing such a nominee was not easy. With 726 votes needed to nominate, the first ballot showed Clark with 440½, Wilson 324, Harmon 148, Underwood 117½, and the rest scattered. On the tenth ballot Clark had a simple majority. Up to this time Nebraska's and Bryan's votes had been for Clark. On the fourteenth ballot Bryan rose to explain that, since a few ballots earlier New York had shifted its votes to Clark, he was changing his vote from Clark to Wilson. The stalemate was prolonged, until Wilson was nominated on the forty-sixth ballot. The Bryan interregnum in the Democratic Party had come to an end.

Wilson's Presidential Party Philosophy

Wilson's two terms in the Presidency failed to heal all the wounds. In fact, some aspects of Wilson's leadership further irritated them and created new ones. Woodrow Wilson was no ordinary man or President.

Not since Madison, Jefferson, Hamilton, and Van Buren had a President concerned himself in his writings with the subject of presidential party leadership as thoughtfully as Wilson. The earlier writers dealt chiefly with the functions of parties as electioneering or congressional organs. Many maintained that Presidents could and should be nonpartisan and that the parties themselves were not entirely legitimate. During Wilson's lifetime, however, particularly when he was a young political science professor at Princeton, parties—and Presidents as party leaders—had come to be accepted features of American life.

Even more significant from Wilson's view, the British had evolved their modern parliamentary party system, a model that Wilson believed admirable. Early in his writings, he compared presidential party leaders with the British Prime Ministers in Parliament and urged that Americans imitate the British institutional arrangements. By the time he became President, Wilson no longer advocated imitation; he apparently *assumed* the two systems to be similar. He conducted the Presidency as though he were a Prime Minister—a grievous misjudgment of the American political process.

Wilson's Cabinet appointments, which included Bryan as Secretary of State, were a mix of party leaders and professional civil servants. Long an advocate of the civil service merit system, Wilson approached the appointment of more than fifty thousand postmasters, district attorneys, collectors of customs, and other officials as a matter for personal review. His first days in the White House were almost totally occupied in this manner until other duties compelled him to return to the practice of congressional recommendations. In the prime ministerial manner, he read his messagess to Congress in person. Eager to cooperate with their first President since Cleveland, congressional Democrats helped make the party caucus into an instrument for the advancement of the presidential program.

Thus, Wilson's progressive domestic program was, for the most part, adopted during the first year and a half of his Administration. The wave of reform legislation reinforced Wilson's impression that strong presidential leadership could give the country a parliamentary system. As World War I began in Europe, Wilson's long "honeymoon" with Congress gave way to the normal practices of party competition and executive-legislative separation.

President Wilson had been elected by a plurality of the major-party votes in 1912. The tripartite character of presidential politics during these years greatly complicated his tenure. His own 6,300,000 votes totaled less than the combined 4,000,000 cast for Roosevelt under the Progressive banner and 3,500,000 for Taft under the Republican. It was never clear how many Roosevelt Progressives might have otherwise been Wilson votes or would subsequently become Wilson supporters. If Roosevelt and Taft were to become reconciled, said many Democratic leaders, there would be serious question that Wilson could be reelected in 1916. These doubts kept other doubts alive; for example, which party leaders would control the national party agencies in the event of defeat?

During Wilson's first term, a generation of young Democrats emerged, devoted to the President and to his brand of progressivism. Chief among these were Franklin D. Roosevelt and William Gibbs McAdoo of New York,[2] Josephus Daniels of North Carolina, Carter Glass of Virginia, Vance McCormick of Pennsylvania, Thomas J. Walsh of Montana, to mention a few. These young Wilsonians frequently found themselves on the other side of party affairs from Charles Murphy of Tammany, Roger Sullivan and George Brennan of Illinois, James Nugent of New Jersey, Tom Taggart of Indiana,

---

[2] McAdoo moved to California in later years.

and Edmund H. Moore of Ohio. The latter were the older generation of professionals whose state organizations and interests were basically conservative or middle-of-the-road.

Another source of political discomfort for the Wilsonians was developments in the southern wing of the party. Although the southern states were solidly Democratic, the Democratic parties within them were far from united. There were the more conservative and moderate congressional elements, represented by men like Underwood. There were the fiery populist remnants of the Bryan era, which, like Bryan himself, were moving more and more in the direction of religious fundamentalism in politics and prohibition. Outside the Democratic Party in the South, but inescapably an influence upon it, was the Ku Klux Klan.

The Klan was a product of the Reconstruction era. It was then organized as a secret society expounding white supremacy and a nativist brand of Americanism. Its organizational activities were again stimulated around 1915 as a reaction to the flood of immigrants coming into this country, the patriotic fervor generated by the World War, and fears of Negro advancement in southern communities. Within a few years, the Klan's membership spread into every state of the Union, achieving a membership of several million. In some states, its leaders either controlled or significantly influenced the decisions of one or the other major party.

By 1916 President Wilson was thoroughly absorbed in the problems of American foreign policy. The country was divided about its relations with the contending powers in Europe, and, for some time, benefited from trade with both sides. Wilson and the nation trod a difficult path between tales of German atrocities on the one hand and the irritations of an illegal British blockade on the other. Economics, culture, and propaganda, however, produced a drift toward the Triple Entente (Great Britain, France, and Russia). As he was placed in nomination in 1916, Wilson was credited with great feats of diplomacy and for "having kept us out of war."

Colonel House, the President's personal adviser, viewed the election campaign essentially as an opportunity to swing as many Roosevelt Progressive votes as possible into the Democratic column. It was a relatively unexciting contest. The President made few speeches. His Assistant Secretary of the Navy, Franklin D. Roosevelt, made many. So did the Republican Roosevelt, whose enmity to Wilson was at times so extreme as to *gain* votes for the President!

The outcome was unbearably close. For a time, as the California returns drifted in, it seemed that Hughes had won. In the last analysis however, Wilson carried California by a few thousand votes—and with it, the Presidency.

On April 6, 1917, the United States declared war against th Central Powers. It was a time of bipartisan cooperation as Wilso called upon the services of eminent Republicans: Herbert Hoover Edward Stettinius, William Howard Taft, and others.

But Wilson's misreading of presidential-congressional politics per sisted. Goaded by Republican Senator Henry Cabot Lodge and con vinced that Allied victories over the Central Powers made his own positions irresistible, the President launched an attack upon th Republican Party during the closing days of the 1918 campaign. Al though the party holding the Presidency invariably lost seats i Congress in the midterm, Wilson insisted, again in the parliamentar manner, upon trying to stem this tendency. Said he:

> If you [the American people] have approved of my leadership an wish me to continue to be your unembarrassed spokesman in affairs a home and abroad, I earnestly beg that you will express yourselves unmis takably to that effect by returning a Democratic majority to both th Senate and the House of Representatives. . . . The return of a Republi can majority to either House of the Congress would . . . certainly b interpreted on the other side of the water as a repudiation of my leader ship.

As for more than a century, however, the party incumbent in th Presidency lost seats in Congress in 1918. Having himself stated th conditions of defeat, the President could hardly escape the implica tions of his own words. Executive-legislative relations deteriorate further when Lodge became Senate floor leader. Together, Lodg and Theodore Roosevelt, old political friends, maintained a politica and personal campaign against Wilson that harassed the President al through the Paris Peace Conference of 1919 and, for that matter, t the end of his term.

Wilson returned from Europe on July 8, 1919, and presented th Peace Treaty, together with its covenant for a League of Nations, t the Senate for ratification. It was a tragic time for such a proposal Republicans controlled Congress, and Lodge controlled the Repub licans. On the pretext that the treaty needed to be revised to protec American sovereignty, Lodge led a dilatory action aimed at humiliat ing Wilson, reasserting legislative ascendancy over the executiv branch, and creating an issue for the 1920 campaign.

Wilson, for his part, insisted that the treaty be ratified exactly as he had presented it. In September he embarked upon a passionate tour of the country in defense of the treaty and the League. Within several weeks, the President suffered a stroke that paralyzed the left half of his body. Thus, during the height of the debate over the League, the President was ill and literally incommunicado. The treaty failed to be ratified, and the nation speculated about Wilson's health and his interest in a third term.

The third term question was to become an integral part of Wilson's fight for the League. The two-term tradition and his illness complicated his strategy. So, also, did the emergence of various claimants to the succession. Indefatigable, Bryan encouraged the formation of "Bryan Leagues." Other candidates were Attorney General A. Mitchell Palmer, noted for his anti-Communist crusade, National Chairman Homer Cummings, Ambassador to England John W. Davis, and Governor James M. Cox of Ohio. McAdoo, now the President's son-in-law, was the object of an anomalous combination of pro-Wilson and anti-Wilson sentiment.

The 1920 national convention met under the poorest conditions of intraparty relations. "Wets" stood against "Drys." Populists stood against conservatives. State bosses stood against Wilsonians. Each set of difficulties coincided with the others. Atop it all was the President's own silence regarding his health, his interest in renomination, and his preference, if any, for a successor. His abdication of party leadership threw the convention into a forty-four-ballot stalemate.

On the first ballot, twenty-four candidates received votes, but only four went over the 100 mark: McAdoo, 266; Palmer, 256; Cox, 134; Smith, 109. Governor Alfred E. Smith was New York's favorite son and a rallying point for the Murphy-Sullivan-Brennan-Taggart alliance. Governor Cox of Ohio, on the other hand, was from the same state as Senator Harding, the Republican nominee. He was also a "Wet," with a good labor record, friendly but not intimately associated with the Wilson Administration, and a Democratic winner in a pivotal and normally Republican state.

Again and again there was discussion at the convention about placing the President's name in nomination, talk that was never explicitly discouraged by Wilson's associates. Whether he would have accepted or not if nominated, Wilson evidently viewed the nomination decision as an occasion for a British-type vote of confidence on his League of Nations policy.

Klan, Catholic, and Compromise

The nomination of Governor Cox was generally interpreted as a defeat for the Wilson Administration. To offer an olive branch to the Wilsonians, the convention chose Franklin D. Roosevelt, an anti-Tammany Wilsonian who was at the same time a good friend of Governor Smith's, for the vice-presidential place.

It was a losing campaign from the start. Division among Democrats and unity among Republicans (Theodore Roosevelt had died a year earlier) would have been sufficient to bring defeat to the party. In addition, though, 1920 was the first presidential year for women's suffrage. The first women to go to the polls, as should have been expected, were those who were normally from the higher educational and economic groups—that is, mainly Republicans.[3] The Harding landslide gave the Republicans a 59–37 margin in the Senate and a 296–135 majority in the House. With it began a twelve-year period of Republican control of the White House.

The vacancy in Democratic presidential party leadership following Cox's defeat and Wilson's retirement brought on a decade of violent factional controversy. Among the main actors in the heated but slow-moving drama were William Gibbs McAdoo, Alfred E. Smith, the southern leadership in Congress, and Franklin D. Roosevelt.

Preparations for the next nominating battle began early. McAdoo, in order to avoid a fight with the New York organization, established residence in California, his candidacy informally supported by various elements in the Klan and the Anti-Saloon League. However, when the McAdoo leaders inaugurated a skirmish over the national chairmanship, congressional Democrats succeeded in gathering a coalition to elect former Representative Cordell Hull.

Hull gave prompt attention to his unwieldy job, particularly noting that "the Republicans got out their women to vote." Under Hull's guidance, the party enjoyed substantial success in the 1922 midterm election, gaining seventy-five seats in the House, thereby reducing the Republican majority to eighteen. Party leaders throughout the nation applauded Hull's achievement, and the Tennessee legislature recommended him for the presidential nomination.

McAdoo's managers stepped up their efforts early in 1923. Henry Ford ranked high among candidate names. Underwood, the candidate

[3] See pp. 23 ff.

f the congressional wing, shortly launched a forthright campaign
gainst the influence of the Ku Klux Klan in presidential politics.
'ammany's Murphy proposed Governor Smith again. He conferred
ith Brennan of Illinois and Duffy of Pennsylvania, and a stop-
IcAdoo combination was born.

Major stimuli to Democratic candidate activity were the scandals
f the Harding Administration, the President's death in August of
923, and the elevation of the colorless "Silent Cal" Coolidge to the
Vhite House. The Teapot Dome investigation might have provided
10re than sufficient ammunition for the 1924 contest against the
Republicans, but the Democrats were apparently more interested in
lefeating each other. McAdoo: a Protestant, Dry, Wilsonian, favorite
•f the Klan (whose support he never disavowed). Smith: a Catholic,
Vet, product of the cities, favorite of the state bosses. In Smith's
orner was Franklin D. Roosevelt, recovering from a year's battle
vith infantile paralysis. The former vice-presidential nominee's name
s Smith's campaign manager added an element of Wilsonian pro-
ressivism to the Governor's cause.

At Madison Square Garden in New York the 1924 convention at-
nosphere was dominated by the Klan's brash declaration of its great
nterest in the party's decision. The Underwood managers promptly
oressed for a plank naming the Klan as a secret society opposed to
he spirit of the Constitution.

The McAdoo managers suggested that the nomination come before
olatform adoption; their proposal lost, 559–513. On the other hand,
he Underwood plank condemning the Klan was defeated $543\frac{3}{20}$
o $542\frac{7}{20}$, a fractional difference that was a measure of the serious-
1ess of the party split. The McAdoo-Smith deadlock lasted for 103
oallots, the last several of these devoted to a slow shift toward a
compromise candidate, John W. Davis of West Virginia. While the
oarty destroyed its election prospects with each succeeding ballot, one
oersonality stood out for his oratorical, managerial, and political skill:
Franklin D. Roosevelt.

Davis suffered a crushing defeat at the hands of President Coolidge.
McAdoo and Smith supporters began to posture themselves for another round in 1928. At this point, Roosevelt exchanged a series of
etters with Senator Walsh, permanent chairman of the 1924 convention, concerning a host of practical organizational problems faced by
the presidential party. Then, in a letter to some three thousand
Democratic leaders, Roosevelt pointed to the archaic aspects of
party organization and solicited their advice for improvement. He was

the only party leader with enough friends to raise so controversial topic. Roosevelt thought that a conference of national party leader would be helpful in gathering together plans. But, William Jennings Bryan was still able to express an opinion, and he joined congres sional leaders in recommending delay. The conference never came off.

Between 1925 and 1927 the Smith managers cautiously built the ties. Pro-Smith leaders captured key positions in Connecticut, Mas sachusetts, New Jersey, Pennsylvania, and states further south along the eastern seaboard. New York City's mayor James J. Walker, the charming "Jimmy," toured the South in search of Smith votes. By late summer of 1927 McAdoo felt the pressure and announced that he was no longer a candidate for the nomination. The national con vention was to be an Al Smith rally.

Governor Smith was the first Catholic to win a major-party nomi nation for the Presidency. He first offered the national chairmanship to Roosevelt, who declined and later ran for governor. The chairman ship position eventually went to a prominent businessman, John J Raskob of General Motors Corporation and long Smith's personal friend. With Andrew Mellon leading much of the business community in support of Herbert Hoover, Governor Smith hoped to counter with Raskob. However, Raskob was not only a businessman but also a Wet, a Catholic, and politically inexperienced. It proved to be a costly selection in a campaign that was bound to have religious overtones The Protestant South, rural and Dry, could hardly swallow the double portion of ingredients it so disliked.

In the election, the Solid South was split, Florida, Texas, and states in the upper South going to Hoover. Across the nation, how ever, Smith pulled the Democratic share of the total vote up from 29 per cent in 1924 to 41 per cent, with particularly large jumps among recently Americanized immigrant groups in the large urban centers and in the states where the 1924 progressives had been strongest Despite the electoral defeat and the high level of prosperity at the start of Hoover's term, Democratic prospects were improving. Within the party, the more embittered factions had over the previous decade eliminated each other. Outside the party, farmers and labor were becoming increasingly active and disenchanted with Republican pol icies. The stock market crash of 1929 and the ensuing Depression— "Hoover's Depression"—reinforced the national shift toward the Democratic column.

CHAPTER 6

Congressional Democrats: A Century of Crises and Contests

BETWEEN 1825 AND 1840, the House of Representatives receded as the chief locus of the national party drama, giving way to the Jacksonian conception of the Presidency. Then, between 1840 and 1860, the main scenes were played in the Senate, where the Great Debates over the federal system, slavery, and executive-legislative powers were conducted and the Great Compromises were hammered out.

Congressional Democrats held majorities, often very large ones, in twelve of the fifteen sessions of the House from 1829 to 1859. But, perhaps because the nation's rapid expansion brought so much new blood into the House membership and in large measure because the party heavyweights were in the Senate, the party-in-the-House made relatively small impact upon national politics during these decades.

In the Senate the size of the Democratic majorities in thirteen of the fifteen sessions was somewhat smaller than in the House. The dramatic political personalities were decidedly more numerous. However, as the decade of the 1850's came to a close, the disappearance of the Whigs, the arrival of the Republicans, the hostility between northern and southern Democrats, all contributed to great confusion in party alignments, often making party labels meaningless.

In fact, the twelve years between 1860 and 1872 witnessed a kind of madness in the legislative party system. The battles that took place in Congress may have been less bloody but were hardly less intense than those on the battlefields. The newly powerful Republicans split into radical and conservative factions. The Radicals employed the halls of Congress to mount attacks upon Lincoln and the Presidency itself, demand the appointment of Republican generals to conduct the war, embark upon impeachment proceedings against the former Democrat who became President upon Lincoln's assassination, surround President Grant with a Senate cabal, and pursue the Reconstruction policies whose consequences have taken the nation nearly a century to adjust to.

Reconstruction of a Nation or Imprisonment of a Party?

The Radical Republicans, led in the Senate by "Zack" Chandler of Michigan and in the House by "Bluff Ben" Wade of Ohio, took a distinctive view of the War between the States and the nature of the peace to be concluded. Whereas Lincoln assumed that the southern states never left the Union, the Radicals, who came to dominate congressional action, insisted that the separation of the sections had been complete and that readmission was to be permitted only under the most stringent conditions. The Radicals were eager to settle the issue on the battlefield and set total victory as their goal.

The effect of some of these conditions was, arithmetically speaking, simple enough. The eleven southern states in the Confederacy had had twenty-two votes in the United States Senate and fifty-eight in the House—nearly all in the Democratic column. So long as the southern Democrats were not among those counted, the Radicals could maintain and advance their control over national politics. Thus, the speakership of the House of Representatives remained in Republican hands until 1875, and the Senate had a Republican majority until 1879.

The lengths to which Radicals were willing to go is perhaps most plainly demonstrated in their treatment of Andrew Johnson, successor to the Presidency upon Lincoln's death.

Johnson, a Democrat when nominated to Lincoln's "Union" ticket, tried to keep his party preference obscure, an attempt that became increasingly untenable as the Radicals began to override his vetoes of their Reconstruction program. Nonetheless, the President refused to commit himself politically beyond urging the election of a pro-Johnson Congress in 1866.

The Congress, in fact, had become something of a political tennis court, the Radicals legislating and the President vetoing one reconstruction measure after the other. After a point, the Radicals were able to mobilize the votes to override these vetoes.

Meanwhile, Senator James R. Doolittle of Wisconsin inaugurated a movement that he hoped would produce a thoroughly Johnsonian political organization. He called an unprecedented midterm national convention, the National Union Convention, for August 16, 1866. The object was to provide a forum for a coalition of War Democrats and conservative Republicans. Great pains were taken to exclude Peace Democrats, and particularly Clement Vallandigham and Fernando Wood. The Radicals responded to this challenge by calling *two* other interim national conventions to be held in Philadelphia at the same time.

The Johnson convention established several committees to work in the off-year congressional campaign. Its National Union Executive Committee consisted of two delegates from each state, territory, and the District of Columbia, but this committee made a minor contribution to the campaign. A nine-member Resident Executive Committee at Washington and a larger Committee on Finance were also chosen, with banker Charles Knapp of New York serving as chairman of both.

Throughout the congressional campaign President Johnson kept in close touch with the Resident Committee. In effect, this was a congressional campaign committee such as exists today. Again the Radicals responded with an organization of their own: the Union Republican Congressional Committee composed of one member representing each state's party delegation from both houses.[1]

In conjunction with the work of the Knapp committee, President Johnson embarked upon his unprecedented "Swing Around the Circle," a tour of the entire country lasting from August 28 to September 16, during which he urged the voters to return a Congress that would support his programs. Odds then, as they are to this day, were against the incumbent President's party (presumably Democratic in Johnson's case) in the congressional midterm election. The Radicals returned as numerous as before but more determined to remove the "enemy" from the office of Chief Executive.

The Vice-Presidency had, of course, remained vacant after Johnson became President. The 1866 election returns were still coming in when John Forney, the Radical Secretary of the Senate, suggested to "Zack" Chandler a plan to put "Bluff Ben" Wade into the position of presiding officer of the Senate, and thus next in line for succession to the Presidency. In order to capture the Presidency itself, Forney advised going ahead with impeachment proceedings against Johnson.[2]

---

[1] Campaign committees in Congress had been in use from time to time ever since the congressional caucus of the early nineteenth century, occasionally operating with prominence in the management of presidential campaigns. The committees developed in 1866 were distinctive because of their midterm character and their permanency as agencies of the parties in Congress.

[2] Forney to Chandler, November 3, 1866, Zachariah Chandler Papers, Library of Congress.

The Radical effort to capture the nation's principal office, as noted in the previous chapter, failed by a one-vote margin.

Party Recovery and Reunion

Although the Democrats were losing in the contests for the Presidency, they did enjoy steady improvement of their congressional position throughout the Grant Administration. Off-year successes in 1874 enabled the Democrats to choose their first Speaker since the beginning of the Civil War, and this they did with unusual care. Samuel J. Randall of Pennsylvania was, for all practical purposes, the leader of House Democrats, but the party chose M. C. Kerr, a congressman with fewer political scars.

Kerr projected a fine image of the party before the nation, as did a vigorous first-term congressman from New York City, Abram Hewitt, son-in-law of the famous Peter Cooper and political associate of Governor Tilden of New York. Tilden and Hewitt had worked together in driving Boss Tweed and the Canal Ring from New York and were now working for Tilden's nomination as a "reform candidate" for President.

Hewitt, serving as Tilden's advance scout in Washington, spoke chiefly on the two issues dividing the Democratic Party at that time: currency and the tariff. Northwestern agrarian elements in the party, reacting to the farm depressions that afflicted their section, had been pushing for a soft-money, greenback currency policy for several years. Eastern business Democrats were firmly for a hard-money policy; this was the position that Hewitt advocated. The tariff issue was also moving to the fore, and Hewitt, an antiprotectionist, favored a tariff for revenue only.

Speaker Kerr died within the year, and Randall was chosen to succeed him. It was Randall who presided during the disputed Hayes-Tilden election. Partisan Democrat though he was, Randall insisted upon following to the letter the procedures set down in the Electoral Commission Act. From December to March no issue absorbed Congress more than the problem of determining which set of election returns in South Carolina, Louisiana, Florida, and Oregon would be counted.

Onto the Electoral Commission to decide the contested returns the Senate placed three Republicans and two Democrats, the House three Democrats and two Republicans, and the Supreme Court two Democratic and two Republican justices, with the fifteenth member—a "nonpartisan"—chosen from the Supreme Court by the other four Justices.

As the Commission made eight-to-seven decisions on each set of returns, what had been a "Democratic compromise" (the special commission) produced a Republican President. Hewitt did salvage something for the Democrats: an indirect Republican commitment that federal troops would be withdrawn from the southern states in question, allowing their return to the Democratic fold.

Speaker Randall continued to hold the chair until the Democrats lost their majority in 1880. He was the first of the modern "strong" Speakers, credited with substantially increasing the influence of the speakership through modifications and interpretations of the rules. Two of Randall's Democratic successors (Carlisle and Crisp) and two Republicans (Reed and Cannon) built upon the precedents established by him.

The era from 1876 to 1896 was highly competitive, giving particular significance to such balance-of-power third-party movements as the Greenbacks and the Populists, significance out of all proportion to the number of their votes. The political judgment of many Democratic leaders came to be swayed by these movements.

Democrats on Money: Hard-Soft, Gold-Silver?

Money issues, in one form or another, consumed the attention of national politicians throughout the remainder of the century. The tariff, a matter that had rested dormant since the days of Clay and Calhoun, was revived when customs receipts increased so rapidly that the Treasury found itself with embarrassing surpluses. Should the surplus fund be used to retire the public debt? Such a move would rocket the market price of government obligations beyond any figure that the Secretary of the Treasury could pay. So Congress turned to such outlays as veterans' pensions, lush rivers and harbors appropriations, and, somewhat more reluctantly, an aid to education program. Basically, however, the issue was whether the tariff should be reduced to a level producing revenue only or be maintained at high levels for the continued protection of American industry from foreign competition.

Most Republicans leaned toward protectionism, although some midwestern Republicans, representing agricultural communities, favored reduction. The Democrats were more evenly divided, Hewitt leading the reductionist cause and Speaker Randall supporting protection. Many eastern Democrats spoke through the voice of Senator Arthur Pue Gorman of Maryland, who classified himself as an "incidental protectionist."

Gorman, like many of his colleagues, was not a protectionist on every commodity. For example, he favored the reduction of tin ore duties, and it was hardly a coincidence that Maryland was one of the major centers of the canning industry of that day. On the other hand, Gorman stood four-square in support of protection for coal, marble, and michromate of potash (more of which was being found in Maryland than in nearly any other place in the world).

Actually, a legislator's position on the tariff depended heavily upon his place of residence. Given the number of places of residence and the number of commodities to be imported or protected against import, the tariff issue remained a great source of confusion in congressional politics.

Monetary policy was closely related. Should a large supply of currency and easy credit be made available to the commerce of the country? Or should credit be given only to the best risks, at high prices, so that the nation's currency circulation could be kept close to the level of the gold and silver supply that constituted its underpinning? Political leaders from the banking centers of the East were for the latter solution. Representatives from the agricultural Midwest and the South were for the former alternative, as farmers not only were among the major buyers of credit but seemed unable to rid themselves of economic depression.

Bimetallism was another aspect of this same currency problem. Proponents of bimetallism argued that if the gold and paper currency were not in sufficient supply to handle the needs of a rapidly growing business and agricultural economy, silver, always in plentiful supply and even more so during the 1880's as mining output in Nevada, Colorado, and other Mountain States increased, ought to become a companion to gold as the specie basis for currency.

Thus it was that almost irresistible pressure was placed upon Democratic leaders in Congress to heed the demands of proponents of easy credit, plentiful currency, silver specie, tariff for revenue only, and the reduction of the federal treasury surpluses. In extreme form, these were the demands of the Greenback Party and the Populists.

The Greenbackers experienced their heyday from 1874 through the next decade, in 1876 running a candidate for President. In the congressional elections of 1878 they pulled more than a million votes. In 1880 the Greenback candidate for President received as much as 3.4 per cent of the popular vote. Greenback strongholds lay in some 306 agricultural counties across about 15 states, the most important of these in the Midwest: Iowa, Kansas, Michigan, Missouri, and Texas.

Although the Greenback Party disappeared after 1884, many of its elements reappeared in the Populist Party of the 1890's. Populism, however, was a somewhat more complicated movement. In some parts of the South, the fiery agrarian populism of new Democratic leaders was the basis for wresting local Democratic organizations from the propertied Bourbon Democratic leaders, producing a Populist faction within the Democratic Party. Often Populists competed with the reviving Democratic Party in such states as Alabama, Georgia, Mississippi, and North Carolina. In certain midwestern areas, particularly in Kansas, the Populists invaded and took over Democratic organizations. The free silver and cheap currency elements had strong roots in Colorado, Idaho, Nevada, and Wyoming, there, too, influencing the Democratic leadership.

Even as populism spread through the halls of Congress, hard-money adherents gained influence in the counsels of President Cleveland. Before long, many southern, midwestern, and mountain Democrats found themselves aligned with Populists against a Democratic Administration whose strength lay in the East. The normal competition between the branches simply accentuated these monetary disagreements.

The Republicans were not unperturbed by their own silverites and pro-Populists. But, ideologically and numerically, the Democrats had most to lose, especially in Congress, were they to ignore populism. This was particularly evident in the South, where leaders such as "Pitchfork Ben" Tillman created alliances with friends among the Populists. Tillman and other southern Democrats were also bent upon extirpating from their region all "Black Republicans" installed during Reconstruction and, if possible, all Bourbon Democrats as well. Cheap money, free silver, and white supremacy were the special political potion offered by these men, a brew that could ferment for a long, long time. As noted in an earlier chapter, one-party constituencies demand little updating of ideological and policy positions. Thus, the pattern for more than four decades of southern Democratic behavior in national politics, particularly in Congress, was cut during this Populist era.

Reviewing the 1892 election results, Democratic leaders noted that a million votes—nearly 9 per cent of the national total—had been cast for Weaver, the Populist nominee. This was a great many voters, for whom "free silver" was a throbbing issue. In the House there were approximately 173 antisilver men, 114 silverites, and 69 doubtfuls. Former Speaker Tom Reed, Tammany's Bourke Cockran, and William L. Wilson eloquently represented the Administration's position favoring repeal. The greatest prosilver speeches came from Representative William Jennings Bryan, supported by Richard P. Bland and Joseph W. Bailey. In the Senate James K. Jones of Arkansas led such eminences as George Vest, Henry M. Teller, Fred T. DuBois, and others. When Cleveland's repeal measure passed, silverite leaders in the Democratic Party, with an ear to their Populist allies, paused to reevaluate their allegiance to the Administration.

These reevaluations became decisive during the battle over tariff legislation in the following year. Representative William L. Wilson was in charge of the Administration's reductionist proposal in the House, and Senator Jones was to shepherd it through the Senate. The House bill, although moderate in its reductions, met stubborn resistance in the Senate, where it was padded with over six hundred amendments. Senator Gorman, whom Cleveland already viewed as a "traitor" for having sought a compromise on the silver repeal bill, was at the head of "the Amenders," whose work converted the Wilson-Jones Bill into the Wilson-Gorman Tariff Act.

As the heat of the debate reached a climax, President Cleveland, in a public letter to Congressman Wilson, denounced the failure of "certain Democrats"—referring to Gorman and his followers—to keep the party's pledges. Gorman delivered a stinging reply from the Senate floor, while Senator Jones sat silent and unwilling to defend the Administration he presumably represented. It was Jones' opinion that Cleveland had sufficient information about the legislative negotiations to have taken a firmer stand privately before resorting to a public fight. The Senate version of the tariff was passed and became law without Cleveland's signature.

The party's factions thus arrived at a crossroads. The President now became a convenient and well-rounded target for all who were riding the tides of discontent. Ben Tillman promised to stick a pitchfork in Cleveland's "old ribs." Missouri's Champ Clark spoke of Cleveland, Benedict Arnold, and Aaron Burr in the same breath. The less violent turned to the more practical problems of presidential and congressional elections in 1896.

The congressional election of 1894 was particularly damaging to the Democrats, who limped into the House of Representatives with only 104 to the Republican's 284 seats. The Populists had produced 1,471,600 votes at the polls, and it seemed that these were the votes that had cost Democratic seats. The one issue that transcended all others in symbolizing popular discontent was "free silver." The issue split both major parties, the Democrats more seriously than the Republicans. An analysis of the resolutions issued by state party conventions and leaders during the spring of 1895 revealed that the Republicans could expect 322 free-silver delegates against 584 sound-money men at their 1896 national nominating convention. The Democrats, on the other hand, might expect 433 silverites against 473 sound-money votes.

Bryan's presidential nomination and defeat in the election against McKinley in 1896 was a less serious blow to the new silverite coalition in the Democratic Party than were the discovery of new gold deposits in the Klondike region and the era of national prosperity that burst forth shortly after the election. The shortage of currency, which had been the major economic justification for the free silver movement, was no longer a pressing problem. But politicians find it difficult to give up old and familiar issues.

Nonetheless new issues pressed in. The Spanish-American War and its outcome made imperialism the grand new issue. The annexation of the Philippines, Puerto Rico and other distant islands was opposed by eminent figures of both parties. The peace treaty with Spain was approved in the Senate by only a single vote more than the necessary two thirds.

Democratic leaders across the country took up discussion of the priority to be given the imperialism issue in their legislative program and in the next presidential election. Had feeling on the free-silver standard abated? Was the growing antitrust sentiment in the country sufficient to be given party recognition? Complicating Democratic deliberation were the well-organized pressure groups that had come upon the American political scene—for example, the bimetallists, the anti-imperialists, the antitrusters, the prohibitionists.

These divisions of opinion and the party's inability to produce a dramatic new national leadership left congressional Democrats a squabbling minority in both houses during the opening decade of the twentieth century.

Administration of the nation's new overseas dependencies proved a sticky and expensive task. Monopoly-dominated industries strained the governing capacities of the states and the cities; demands for federal intervention became increasingly vociferous. Muckrakers in the press and congressional investigating committees found much to criticize.

Still unaccustomed to its emerging role as a world power, the nation hesitatingly gave attention to defense needs, particularly an enlarged Navy—never forgetting the relationship between arms production and domestic prosperity. As populism faded, progressivism took its place. Anti-imperialism became tinged with isolationism. Antimonopolism acquired the sharpness of marxist idiom. Hostility to corruption and whiskey became associated with demands for such governmental reforms as the city-manager system, primary elections, women's suffrage, and direct election of senators.

Wilson's "Parliamentary" System

In the antimonopoly spirit of the day, House Democrats in 1910 composed the main phalanx in a revolt against the monopoly powers that had accumulated in the office of Speaker. As chairman of the Committee on Rules the Speaker had, in addition to his prerogative of floor recognition, that committee's powers for programming the day-to-day business of the House. Under Speaker "Uncle Joe" Cannon, these powers became a personal rather than a party tool. The Republican caucus had been practically dispensed with by Cannon, and a small group of 30 progressive Republicans could do little against the more than 180 other Republicans who kept Cannon in office. Led by Congressman Champ Clark of Missouri, Democrats united to trim the Speaker's office.

On March 17, 1910, Representative George W. Norris of Nebraska, a progressive Republican, offered a resolution calling on the House, rather than the Speaker, to appoint a Committee on Rules, excluding the Speaker from membership thereon. Two days later, the resolution was adopted, 191 to 155, every Democrat and about 30 progressive Republicans voting for it. It was a spectacular victory.

The Democrats, who assumed control in the next session, revived their own caucus as an instrument of party management. Democratic majorities in the elections of 1910 put Champ Clark into the speakership, where he gained sufficient popularity to make him the leading contender for the Democratic presidential nomination in 1912. I was Woodrow Wilson, however, who received that nomination. Despite his own election as a minority President, Wilson swept a large

Democratic majority into the House along with enough Democratic senators to control the upper chamber.

Having just gained control of the two elective branches of government, Democrats were for a time willing to follow the vigorous President in his governmental experiments. Not since Washington and Adams, for example, had a President addressed Congress in person. Wilson revived the practice as a symbolic affirmation of his conception of presidential party leadership.

Wilson actively used the recently revived Democratic House caucus, giving it the ordinarily impossible task of working out a basic revision of the tariff. Working through the caucus, where the two-thirds rule governed, Wilson was able to place before the House a bill that won by an overwhelming majority without encountering the usual revisionist tactics. Then, from a vantage point in the President's Room just off the Senate chamber, Wilson maneuvered Senate Democrats into conducting a caucus of their own on the bill. This rare conclave subsequently declared the tariff bill to be a party measure, and it was passed.

Democratic cohesion thus established, there followed a series of major legislative actions. Banking and monetary reform came through the Owen-Glass Federal Reserve Act of 1913, despite the objection of the banking industry. Growing malpractices of the industrial monopolies were dealt with in the Clayton Anti-Trust Act of 1914, which specifically exempted labor and farmer organizations from its requirements. The Federal Trade Commission was created to look after the provisions of the Clayton Act. The Newlands Act improved the arbitration process in railway labor disputes. Federal farm loan banks were created to improve the extension of credit to farmers.

But a honeymoon does not a system of government remake. Wilson, for example, did not feel a need to carry his conception of leadership into the congressional and local election campaigns. Unlike the parliamentary system, *his* office did not depend on this. Thus, during the winter of 1913 when state legislatures were for the last time choosing a third of the membership of the United States Senate, Wilson let pass opportunities to develop Democratic-Progressive alliances. The following year National Chairman McCombs, with whom Wilson subsequently severed relations, made unusual arrangements for a midterm campaign effort run jointly by the national committee and the congressional campaign committee. Wilson expressed a wish to take the stump in behalf of Democratic congressional candidates in 1914, but the death of the first Mrs. Wilson late that summer prevented his doing so. He limited himself to letter-writing instead, and some Democrats viewed this as a rather severe reduction of presidential effort. Although the Democrats maintained a majority, they lost fifty-eight seats. Both the presidential and congressional elections in 1916 were near-ties.

World War I drew to an end in October, 1918, and Wilson promptly levied his famous attack upon the Republican Party in Congress. When Democrats lost control of both houses in November, congressional Democrats became reluctant to follow a party leader who seemed so divorced from the realities of American politics.

Congressional Democrats had another reason for retreating from the Wilson banner: the southern wing, deeply entrenched in one-party districts at home, was clearly to be a major source of national party leadership in the coming decade or more. The following table illustrates the point.

Southern Democratic Strength Among Congressional Democrats, 1918–1936

Year	House of Representatives So. Dems./Total Dems.	Senate So. Dems./Total Dems.
1918	114/191	26/47
1920	107/131	26/37
1922	115/206	26/43
1924	115/183	26/39
1926	116/195	26/46
1928	103/163	26/39
1930	117/220	26/47
1932	116/310	26/60
1934	117/319	26/69
1936	116/331	26/76

The southern Democratic contingent was large and stable. From 1918 to 1930, inclusive, southern representatives constituted more than half the Democratic strength in the House. In the Senate, the proportion of southerners among the Democrats was even greater. With the imminent departure of Bryan and Wilson from the national political scene, it would have been surprising if southerners had not insisted upon exercising their preponderant weight in national party affairs. Not until 1932, when the New Deal swept a substantial nonsouthern Democratic majority into both houses, could southern Democrats be considered a minority within the congressional party.

Era of Party Division and National Withdrawal

President Wilson returned from the Paris Peace Conference to present to the Senate a peace treaty containing arrangements for a League of Nations. The treaty failed by a vote of 53–58, its failure marking the beginning of a decade of rejection. The nation, deeply wounded by its first participation in a major international war, turned to isolationism. The plaints of the debt-ridden farmers were rejected as prosperity prevailed among nearly every other economic group in the country. Prohibition, put into the Constitution in 1917, was rejected by a high-living nation in which organized crime reaped the largest harvest. Traditional American toleration was challenged frontally as the Ku Klux Klan and other nativist groups infiltrated the political parties to resist the Americanization of the recently arrived millions from overseas. The Democratic Party was also rejected in election after election, as much for the divisions within its ranks as for its lack of program and national leadership.

Congressional Democrats became the caretakers of the party after the defeat of 1920, promoting Representative Cordell Hull from the chairmanship of the congressional campaign committee to the chairmanship of the national committee. Under Hull's direction the midterm congressional campaign of 1922, again conducted as a combined effort of the national and congressional committees, managed to add seats to the Democratic side in the lower house.

Another hard-hitting campaign was launched by Senator Thomas J. Walsh, whose investigations broke the Teapot Dome oil scandal of the Harding Administration. Harding's death in August and Coolidge's legislative defeats at the hands of a Republican cabal in the Senate seemed to promise a Democratic revival in 1924.

But the ingredients of victory were not really present. The Klan issue destroyed Underwood. Anti-Wilson sentiment ended the chances of the late President's son-in-law, McAdoo. The Drys halted Al Smith's march. Defeat came to the Democrats in both the presidential and congressional races.

During the 1920's former Roosevelt Progressives gathered some of the bitter fruit of agricultural discontent, emerging as La Follette Progressives or Farmer-Laborites and preparing many of the policy proposals that later matured under the New Deal. In the main, agrarian and labor disaffection was given voice by small groups of progressives in each of the major parties in Congress. Their legislative proposals sought to alleviate unemployment, outlaw child labor, introduce old-age pensions, promote slum clearance, and, in the McNary-Haugen bill, stabilize farm prices and reduce agricultural surpluses through a program of federal purchases.

By 1926 some forty Democrats, five Republican insurgents (Norris, Howell, Nye, Frazier, and La Follette) voting consistently with the Democrats, and one Farmer-Laborite began to challenge the Republican senatorial majority. Such progressives as Borah of Idaho, Hiram Johnson of California, and Couzens of Michigan held the pivotal Republican votes. The alliance was able to pass the McNary-Haugen bill, but within a week it was vetoed by Coolidge. The time for progressivism had not yet arrived. The country raced along on its cycle of prosperity and inflation.

Midwestern progressives, led by Senator Borah, had for years blamed the chronic agricultural depression of the 1920's upon "inadequate" tariff protection for farm products. Thus, progressives joined with manufacturers and labor leaders in demanding high tariffs. President Hoover, anticipating only moderate adjustments, agreed to call a special session of Congress in April, 1929, for purposes of tariff revision. Democratic leaders, with somewhat greater foresight, predicted substantial difficulty between the President and leaders of his own party in Congress and issued a statement promising him their cooperation. After months of legislative turmoil, by a Senate vote of 49 to 47 Republicans produced the Hawley-Smoot Tariff, the highest tariff wall erected by any government to that date. Not even the stock market crash of October 29, 1929, constrained the isolationism of congressional Republicans.

As the Depression worsened, Democrats regained control of the House for the first time since 1919 and put John Nance Garner of Texas into the Speaker's chair. In the Senate, however, each party held forty-eight seats. President Hoover suggested that the Democrats be permitted to organize the Senate, but after several ballots, the Republicans did. It was a pyrrhic victory; congressional Democrats devoted the session to preparations for the next national campaign.

Following his defeat in the presidential race, Al Smith endorsed the concept of a full-time permanent national headquarters for the party. His national chairman, multimillionaire John J. Raskob, was able to produce the financial resources to create for the first time such a headquarters. The staff's main duties were organization, publicity, and research. The research bureau was to prepare documentary materials not only for the publicity bureau at headquarters but, unprecedentedly, for the information of members of Congress. National Chairman Raskob, somewhat prematurely, expressed the opinion that perhaps "the Senatorial and Congressional committees would finally be brought into one organization." [3]

Raskob's efforts were admittedly designed to preserve a national rostrum for Al Smith. But several southern states, such as North Carolina, Texas, Virginia, had voted for Hoover. One thing that aggravated the southerners was the fact that Raskob, Smith's national chairman, was also a Catholic. There were other grounds for southern hostility. The agrarian South saw in the working-class Smith and the capitalist Raskob a strange alliance against the farmer. Nor did southern Drys welcome Smith-Raskob proposals for the modification of Prohibition.

Southerners in Congress turned to one of their most dignified and experienced national politicians, Cordell Hull, now the United States Senator from Tennessee. In his own words: "In the years following 1928, I strove hard but without particular publicity to organize members of the Democratic National Committee and important Democratic leaders generally, against control of the Democratic Party by Governor Smith and his associates in 1932." [4]

Hull particularly resisted Smith-Raskob plans for national committee preparation of an interim statement on party platform positions. According to Hull, the Democratic national committee "has no authority, expressed or implied, to prescribe issues for the Democratic rank and file of the nation," an attitude which would be reiterated on other significant occasions by congressional Democrats.

Governor Franklin D. Roosevelt, in a "Dear Al" letter to Smith, came to the support of the Hull position: "Historically," Roosevelt said, "the National Committee has always recognized that in between conventions, the spokesmen on policy matters are, primarily, the Democratic Members of the Senate and House of Representatives, together with individuals high in the Party Councils, who, however, speak as individuals. . . ." [5]

In February, shortly after Roosevelt declared himself a candidate for the presidential nomination, Hull withdrew his own favorite-son candidacy. Former National Chairman Homer S. Cummings assumed the duties of liaison between the Roosevelt staff and the congressional

[3] *The New York Times,* May 1, 1929.
[4] *The Memoirs of Cordell Hull* (New York: Macmillan, 1948), I, p. 141.
[5] Elliot Roosevelt, *F.D.R.: His Personal Letters, 1928–1945* (New York: Duell, Sloan and Pearce, 1950), II, p. 179.

Democratic leaders and was especially effective in his talks with Senator Connally of Texas concerning the favorite-son status of Speaker Garner. These talks laid the groundwork for Garner's famous withdrawal in favor of Roosevelt at the 1932 nominating convention.

Thus, another presidential nomination was hammered together in the Congress. It was partially upon the basis of this consensus among legislative Democrats, achieved even before his landslide election, that Roosevelt enjoyed "one hundred days" of almost complete Congressional support of his emergency measures. Further, the Roosevelt landslide pulled in a Congress in which two thirds of the seats were occupied by Democrats.

The New Deal in Congress

The legislative achievements of the first New Deal Congress marked pathways of national policy never before taken. No session of Congress had worked as hard. From thirteen to seventeen million employable Americans were without jobs. Over fourteen thousand banks had failed during 1932. Farmers were destitute as their harvests lay rotting. With the economic system failing, the viability of the political system was also in question. Democrats had the clear responsibility for salvaging both.

New Deal measures poured into the congressional hopper, many of them poorly drafted and hastily enacted in an atmosphere of emergency and near-revolution. The Agricultural Adjustment Act introduced price supports and crop reduction procedures for farm products. An emergency farm mortgage financing plan was designed to halt foreclosures. A securities exchange bill sought to restore confidence in the stock market. The National Industrial Recovery Act provided for organized labor's right of collective bargaining, over $3 billion in public works, and the development of codes of fair competition among stagnated industrial enterprises.

The Civilian Conservation Corps took hundreds of thousands of young men off the bread lines and put them onto long-neglected projects for conserving the nation's natural resources. Because attention to starvation and destitution could not wait, the Federal Emergency Relief Administration began dispensing $500 million in direct relief through state and local agencies. An Emergency Banking Act led to arrangements for safeguarding bank deposits and improving the currency supply. Anticipating the repeal of Prohibition, a beer and wine act was passed. The Muscle Shoals and Tennessee Valley Develop ment Act created the Tennessee Valley Authority and launched a great and successful experiment in regional planning.

In all this legislative hubbub, it was literally impossible for 60 Democratic senators and 310 Democratic representatives to keep in touch, let alone exert concerted political influence upon the Roosevelt program. To cope with the problem, the Democratic House caucus modified its whip system by dividing the nation into fifteen geographical districts, the Democratic congressmen from each electing an assistant whip. These new channels of communication gave congressional Democrats cohesion and direction during these turbulent times.

The midterm congressional election of 1934 was the first in American history in which the party of an incumbent Administration gained rather than lost seats in Congress. The number of Democrats in the Senate rose to 69, in the House to 319. Perhaps an even more significant consequence of this unusual election was the realization by many southern Democrats that they faced the risk of becoming a fading minority in the party they had so recently led.

This fear was further justified by a quiet but fundamental step taken at the 1936 Democratic national convention; the two-thirds nominating rule was changed to a simple majority arrangement. The South, which had been able to veto unacceptable presidential candidates, could no longer do so. Southern Democrats could hardly accept this course of events without a battle. The occasion for such a battle presented itself soon enough in another stronghold of southern strength: the Senate.

A hostile Supreme Court had been invalidating a number of the New Deal measures. Heartened by his overwhelming electoral support in 1936, President Roosevelt, in his Annual Message of 1937, expressed concern over the impasse between the executive and judicial branches. Then, in February, without consulting or forewarning Democratic leaders in Congress, he sent to the Senate a series of recommendations for a general reorganization of the judiciary from the Supreme Court down to the district courts. A key part of his proposal was a provision to add an additional judge to any federal court in which a sitting judge, having reached the retirement age of seventy, did not avail himself of the opportunity to retire on a pension. With six of the nine members of the Supreme Court over seventy, it was easy to interpret the proposal as a "court-packing plan." Looking back over the years, one of Roosevelt's closest advisers, Judge Rosenman, referred to the plan as "the most controversial proposal Roosevelt ever made during his twelve years as President," and one that "cost him much in prestige, particularly in party prestige." [6]

Others saw the Supreme Court proposal as a test of party control. The Republican strategy, guided by Senator Borah, was to let Democrats carry on the entire fight both for and against. The non–New Dealers in the party, particularly those from the South, quickly saw an opportunity to remind a popular President that there were *three* branches in the national government and a *southern interest* in the Democratic Party. Ironically, because of the seniority aspects of congressional organization, Majority Leader Joseph T. Robinson of Arkansas, Pat Harrison of Mississippi, and James F. Byrnes of South Carolina—all southerners—were responsible for carrying the legislative ball for the President's court plan. Opponents of the bill adopted a strategy of delay, to permit events, some quite unexpected, to unfold and public opinion to materialize.

Supreme Court decisions, made many months earlier, began to be announced, as though in response to the pressures of the court plan, in favor of New Deal legislation. Justice VanDevanter, a persistent anti–New Dealer, announced his retirement in June. The least expected and most shocking development was the sudden death of Majority Leader Robinson on June 13, removing the most skillful arbiter of a very difficult battle.

The leadership fight that followed Robinson's death placed in broad daylight the deep split in the Senate's Democratic majority. The two candidates were Pat Harrison of Mississippi and Alben Barkley of Kentucky. The contest was close and the outcome decided only when the President indirectly endorsed Barkley in a famous "Dear Alben" note. This fight, however, cost Roosevelt his court plan, which was rejected shortly thereafter.

Before the year ended, Roosevelt, ordinarily a masterful politician, felt a great need to reassert his party leadership. With the usual patronage largely disposed of and the other resources of the emergency programs decreasingly available, he found, as had Wilson, that the tools of presidential influence over fellow partisans in Congress were few indeed. One "tool" never overtly and directly used was presidential endorsement of or opposition to candidates in his party's primaries.

[6] Samuel I. Rosenman, *Working With Roosevelt* (New York: Harper, 1952), p. 147.

Nonintervention by "outsiders" into state and local contests among fellow partisans (other than in the most subterranean fashion) has been one of the unwritten rules of American politics. However, as the 1938 midterm election approached, Roosevelt adopted a plan for intervening in certain Democratic primaries to give support to New Dealers wherever they were clearly matched against more conservative Democrats. As he put it in his "fireside chat" of June 24, 1938:

As the head of the Democratic Party, however, charged with the responsibility of carrying out the definitely liberal declaration of principles set forth in the 1936 Democratic platform, I feel that I have every right to speak in those few instances where there may be a clear issue between candidates for a Democratic nomination involving these principles, or involving a clear misuse of my own name.

That fall, President Roosevelt lent his support to the primary election opponents of Senator Walter George of Georgia, Senator Millard Tydings of Maryland, and Representative John J. O'Connor of New York. The "Purge," as it was called, succeeded only in the latter instance. Further embarrassing Roosevelt's party leadership were Republican gains of eighty-two seats in the House and eight seats in the Senate.

The Congresses of Roosevelt's second term, although increasingly reluctant to endorse his programs, did establish the Farm Security Administration, which provided loans to tenant farmers; the United States Housing Authority, for extending loans to local governmental housing agencies; a minimum-wage law; and a plan for soil conservation payments to farmers who agreed to restrict production of specific crops.

As the recession of 1938 mounted, Congress found itself again putting millions into public works appropriations. One other kind of appropriation began to assume significant proportions as well: defense spending. A war was brewing in Europe.

War and Peace: A New Era and New Issues

The disenchantments of World War I left the nation isolationist and antiwar. President Roosevelt, long before Pearl Harbor (December 7, 1941), proposed that the United States lease or sell essential war supplies to Britain as a gesture of friendship and a measure for the defense of this country. The "Lend-Lease" debate in Congress was a searching one. It proved to be an indispensable precursor of subsequent defense legislation and repeal of the Neutrality Act. The attacks on Pearl Harbor brought the United States into the war against the Axis.

Although Congress was willing to support its wartime leader in every respect, some Democrats with a longer sense of history looked back over the nation's experience in previous wars and forward to the balance sheet of the Democratic record after World War II. One of these was Senator Harry S. Truman of Missouri. In the Mexican War, the Civil War, the Spanish-American War, and World War I, Truman recalled, sudden and large increases in federal spending for military and related equipment and services had placed the handling of public funds and resources at the mercy of the inefficient, the dishonest, and the greedy. Truman also recalled Lincoln's bitter experience with the Radical Republicans' Committee on the Conduct of the War. It was risky and difficult for a congressional investigating committee, even one of the President's own party, to serve as a "friendly watchdog"—the words were contradictory—in the surveillance of defense spending.

Nonetheless, in February, 1941, Truman recommended the creation of such a committee, of which he became chairman. With an initial fund of only $15,000, and with the earnest purpose of flushing out waste and corruption without embarrassing the Roosevelt war leadership, the Truman committee set about its task. Its investigations produced masses of information about slovenly administration, incompetence, and dishonesty in defense expenditures. Without fanfare, the committee poked around in factories and through military installations. In the several years of its efforts, the Truman committee was conservatively credited with saving the federal government some $15 billion. Senator Truman's fiscal accomplishment and his political tact earned him the gratitude of Democrats and Republicans alike, but in particular the appreciation of President Roosevelt.

World War II set governmental funds and resources in motion at a rate never before experienced by any nation. Upwards of $400 billion poured out of the Treasury for the war effort. Armaments were created and expended without stint. To the 1,100 combat planes available before the war, the nation added nearly 300,000 before the end of the war. Slightly over 1,000 tanks were supplemented by over 80,000. During the first three years, some 45 million bombs were manufactured. The most dramatic of these were produced by the Manhattan Project, a scientific collaboration costing over $2 billion and ushering in the atomic era.

Mechanization of southern agriculture and the labor shortage in northern war plants started a migration that placed over a million southern Negroes into northern communities. Political aspiration followed close upon economic betterment of these migrants, particularly as Democratic urban political organizations such as Daley's in Chicago enlisted the new voters and offered them a part in the nation's decisions such as they had been deprived of for generations. When the war ended, additional millions of Negroes returning from the armed forces settled in the North rather than the South; the Negro "swing vote" in large pivotal urban states became an irrepressible factor in national politics, and the struggle for racial civil rights gathered momentum.

World War II was concluded under the leadership of Harry S. Truman, elevated to the Presidency upon the death of Roosevelt in 1945. The nation had become the most powerful in the world, the most unscathed, the most affluent, and the most teaming with old and new social and political interests. These many interests were, as usual, represented in Congress. Their rapidly shifting postwar claims were juggled gingerly by a body of legislators suddenly released from years of constraint under the Roosevelt "presence" and the demands of a world war.

As Republicans tried to develop election issues, southern Democrats moved to reestablish their old ascendancy in the party. As farmers, workers, businessmen, and other groups sought to protect their New Deal and wartime gains, President Truman fell into wrangles with one after the other of them. When nearly every economic group in the country wanted to make a quick killing through the removal of price and rent controls, Democrats in Congress helped the President hold the line. One of the most controversial pieces of legislation was the Full Employment Act of 1946, for the first time in the history of the American free enterprise system making it the explicit responsibility of the federal government to guard the nation against economic depressions.

But Democratic majorities in Congress could not last forever. Truman's "do-nothing" Eightieth Congress was Republican, and it did something: passed the Taft-Hartley Act over a presidential veto. Organized labor never worked so hard for a ticket as it did for Truman's in 1948. When Truman returned to the White House, congressional Democrats also returned to majority status.

As it had many times before, the nation approached the postwar world with a policy of self-disarmament and economic retrenchment.

But the world and the nation were very different from ever before. A nuclear power cannot hide or isolate itself. Nations, such as the Soviet Union and Communist China, with programs for producing the millennium tomorrow cannot rest. Former allies, devastated by war, cannot face the frontiers of discontent without a helping hand.

The Truman Administration and its Congresses soon found themselves reinstating defense appropriations, signing treaties, and extending foreign economic and military aid. The United Nations Treaty was approved. The Truman Doctrine, giving $400 million in aid to Greece and Turkey, set a precedent. Months later the Marshall Plan inaugurated a program of aid to Europe which, within a decade, reached upward of $33 billion, admittedly a fraction of the cost of conducting a war to salvage Europe. In 1948 Congress endorsed the outlays for the Berlin airlift, this nation's first military confrontation with the Communists. That, too, was cheap when compared with the price of Munich in 1938 and the wars it led to. Congress also provided funds for the Point Four program of technical assistance to new nations and in 1949 put a billion dollars on the line to help build the new North Atlantic Treaty Organization (NATO), twelve nations joined into a formidable shield against the Soviet Union.

The Cold War was something new in international politics. For those reluctant to seek out the Communists abroad, however, there were the investigators at home. Senator Joseph McCarthy, a Wisconsin Republican, set the tone of the 1950 congressional elections and of the era that bears his name by launching a flamboyant crusade against "Communist spies" within our borders, particularly within the State Department and other federal agencies. Where Franklin Roosevelt's "Purge" had failed to unseat Maryland's Millard Tydings, the McCarthy-type campaign did. Republicans, united around a bargain-basement anti-Communism, made impressive gains in 1950 and kept warm the domestic anti-Communist crusade in campaigns over the ensuing decade.

Congressional versus Presidential Democrats

In the halls of Congress Democrats were manufacturing troubles for themselves. Organized crime had become one of the nation's biggest businesses, and Senator Estes Kefauver of Tennessee embarked upon an investigation of crime that took him to the doorstep of some fellow Democrats in local and state politics. Still rankling from Truman's surprise victory of 1948, many southern Democrats proposed Senator Richard Russell of Georgia as the southern candidate for 1952. With Kefauver and Russell factions stalemated, the Adlai Stevenson nomination came as a happy compromise.

Despite an Eisenhower landslide, Republicans in Congress took control by a single vote margin in the Senate and by less than a dozen seats in the House. Senator Russell promptly observed that Stevenson's "titular leadership" meant "title without authority." Democratic policy would be determined in Congress over the following four years! And under the leadership of an unusual team of Texans: Senator Lyndon B. Johnson and House Minority Leader Sam Rayburn.

Johnson, a product of the New Deal era, was a Rayburn protégé and a tireless legislator. Within a short time the country witnessed a popular Republican President in 1954, 1956, and 1958 serving with both houses of Congress under the leadership of a powerful Democratic team. The 1954 election made Rayburn Speaker and Johnson Majority Leader. The Rayburn-Johnson legislative strategy became known as "responsibility in opposition." With the Eisenhower Administration practicing what Professor Walter Johnson called a "politics of postponement," there was, of course, little for congressional Democrats to oppose.

Adlai Stevenson and his national chairman, Paul Butler, however, persisted in advocating the development of distinctive Democratic policy positions. An "information gap" developed between the Democratic titular leader and the congressional leaders. Stevenson nevertheless received an overwhelming majority at the 1956 national convention.

The vice-presidential position was contested by an unusual number of Democratic senators: Estes Kefauver, Hubert H. Humphrey, Albert Gore, John F. Kennedy, and others. The prize went to Senator Kefauver and the glory to Senator John F. Kennedy, son of Joseph P. Kennedy. The young senator was catapulted into the presidential arena on this occasion.

Shortly after the reelection of the Republican President and another Democratic Congress in 1956, Senator Humphrey predicted that the party leadership "will be essentially congressional." And Majority Leader Johnson pointedly observed that "Mr. Stevenson can speak for himself."

Johnson also predicted a continuation of the "responsible opposition" strategy: "We are a good and reasonable group of men working for the good of the country without parties, labels or cliques." When questioned about the need to develop a distinctive Democratic Party program, Johnson added: "No, we'll wait for the President. We'll support him when he's right and oppose him when he's wrong."

Liberal Democrats from the Northeast, upper Midwest, and the Far West were quick to disagree. Led by Senators Humphrey of Minnesota and Douglas of Illinois, this minority developed plans for carving out a distinctive Democratic program, particularly in the civil rights field. As a necessary step towards civil rights legislation, these liberals announced a full-scale assault upon the filibuster rule. When this was interpreted as part of a plan to remove Johnson from the leadership, Senators Kennedy and Humphrey issued emphatic denials, hailing Johnson as the only man skillful enough to lead the party in the Senate. Here indeed was a Senate team to be watched.

As keeper of the Senate's timetable, Majority Leader Johnson was able to give certain colleagues valuable opportunities for demonstrating capacity for leadership. Senator Humphrey was allowed to make the liberal case against the filibuster rule in connection with the strategy to pass civil rights legislation. When the issue was joined, the filibuster rule remained but, under Johnson's direction, a compromise was reached that brought out of Congress the first civil rights legislation in eighty-five years.

When Senator Kennedy initiated a minimum wage bill and other legislation designed to eliminate the racketeering in certain labor unions discovered during his recent Senate investigations, a series of antilabor amendments was tagged onto the Kennedy-Ervin bill and passed by the margin of 47–46. Again Senator Johnson stepped in to arrange compromises, this time watering down the punitive character of some of the amendments. Senator Kennedy came out of the fracas, however, having fully demonstrated to liberal and labor leaders that, although an investigator of unions and the son of one of the nation's wealthiest men, he was also safely on the side of labor's best interests.

Still another presidential candidate was Senator Stuart Symington of Missouri, an established authority on military policy. As another expert on military policy was resident in the White House, Symington's criticisms of Eisenhower military budget requests had particular point. Minority Leader Johnson gave Symington every opportunity to make this point.

The inquiries by the Rayburn-Johnson Congress into the defense positions of the nation were spurred by widespread and excited world response to Sputniks I and II during the closing months of 1957. The

Soviet Union, so often perceived in the press as a backward peasant people, had beaten the most highly industrialized nation in the world by placing in orbit around the earth the first of the man-made satellites.

A period of American self-examination followed, as did a reversal of the Eisenhower economy program in defense spending. This Democratic Congress initiated the pattern of research and development appropriations that carried the United States from the atomic era to the Space Age. The space industry replaced public works and the manufacture of military weapons as the principal type of public spending. In a few short years a Democratic President (Kennedy) would request the resources necessary to land the first man on the moon. Space, both literally and figuratively, began to give American politics a new dimension.

As 1960 approached, several Democratic senators—Johnson, Kennedy, Humphrey, Symington—were again at the forefront of the candidate stable. Majority Leader Johnson, on January 7, 1959, just prior to President Eisenhower's annual message to Congress, delivered his own State of the Union address, in which he cast broadsides against "the burden of laggard government." The undeclared truce between the Republican President and the Democratic Congress came to an end as all hands prepared for the rough political seas of 1960.

"Senators" in the White House

When Senator Kennedy won the presidential nomination over the challenges of Senators Johnson, Humphrey, and Symington, he promptly named Majority Leader Johnson as his running mate. Few observers could miss the political trend: the Democratic Party in Congress had produced a new generation of national leaders.

As President-elect, Kennedy promptly assumed the initiative in preparing for the next session of Congress, in which Democrats had a slightly reduced House majority. Kennedy took a hand in the promotion of Senators Mike Mansfield to Majority Leader and Hubert Humphrey to Democratic Whip. Using innumerable consultants and "task forces," the President-elect pulled together bills, messages, and a State of the Union address. The first great legislative test for the new Administration, however, came not in the choice of leaders or the presentation of programs but rather in the composition of the House Rules Committee, the keeper of the legislative agenda.

The Rules Committee was headed by Howard W. Smith of Virginia, abetted by a coalition of Republicans and southern Democrats. Only Speaker Sam Rayburn could be considered a more seasoned political infighter than Smith, and it was indeed a coup for Kennedy when "Mr. Sam" assumed leadership of a move to "pack" the Rules Committee with three additional members, of whom two would be Democrats friendlier to the President's program. The battle over the powers of the Rules Committee chairman took on the proportions of the 1910 revolt against Speaker Cannon. Rayburn, Kennedy, Johnson, members of the Cabinet, and the White House staff worked long and diligently. Even at that, the change was adopted by the narrow margin of 217 to 212, removing a substantial obstacle to the Kennedy program.

That program during the first half year had approximately three hundred items, of which sixteen were given particular priority. The President's congressional associates were working with small margins, particularly in the House. Legislation was slow in coming, but it did come forth: the Peace Corps, designed to give American youth an opportunity to help the people of less developed nations; the Alliance for Progress, a ten-year program aimed at raising Latin American living standards; unemployment compensation; minimum wage legislation.

The nation and the Democratic Party lost one of their strongest and steadiest hands with the passing of Speaker Rayburn in late 1961. "Mr. Sam" had been Speaker or Minority Leader since 1940, two decades of service and political craftsmanship having few equals in American history. John McCormack, long a competitor of the Kennedys in Massachusetts politics, succeeded to the speakership.

After a relatively unproductive year, members of Congress turned to their 1962 fall election activities, only to have plans and prospects thoroughly shaken by the discovery of Soviet missiles in Cuba. The American "quarantine" of Cuban waters at the end of October had predictable consequences for the election: all incumbents, Democratic and Republican alike, were beneficiaries of the sudden surge of national cohesion. Only in 1934, the height of the New Deal era, did an incumbent Administration do as well in holding or gaining seats in Congress. Four additional seats were won by the Democrats in the Senate, and the party returned almost exactly its previous majority in the House.

The year 1963 brought events that profoundly affected the nation. It opened with President Kennedy's proposals for a $13.6 billion tax cut, greater aid to education, and hospital insurance for the aged through social security. Repercussions followed the admission of James H. Meredith, a Negro, to the University of Mississippi. The racial crisis burst forth again in May, 1963, when dogs and firehoses were used to disperse Negroes in Birmingham, Alabama, during civil rights demonstrations. It was a summer of rioting, bombings, arrests, federal troop movements, and martyrdom. President Kennedy, amidst it all, requested of Congress extensive civil rights legislation, particularly in the areas of equal rights in employment and voting prerogative.

On November 22, 1963, the President was assassinated in Dallas, Texas. Hardly recovered from the shock, congressional Democrats felt the pressure of a familiar hand—Lyndon B. Johnson's. A master of the legislative process, President Johnson once again demonstrated that skill, without public fanfare, in the early months of his Administration. He broke an $11 billion tax-cut bill out of a committee chaired by Senator Byrd of Virginia by first demonstrating his capacity to economize—that is, by taking approximately $5 billion off the Kennedy budget. He further appeased the economy-minded Virginian by consulting with him about the budget message before it was sent and by later thanking him for his cooperation in a national TV speech announcing the tax cut. He worked a similar miracle by getting off the ground and through the Congress his own antipoverty legislation calling for over $900 million for a collection of small programs designed to inaugurate several attacks upon the "pockets of poverty" that persist in the world's most affluent nation.

Probably the most controversial and politically significant piece of legislation in that presidential year was the Civil Rights Bill. Involved at every stage of its movement through the Congress, Johnson nevertheless gave the largest public role to his long-time associate and sometimes opponent, Majority Whip Hubert Humphrey. The southern filibusterers were given a seventy-five-day opportunity to show their constituents how stubbornly they had fought. Humphrey also made clear how stubborn would be the nearly two-thirds majority in the Senate. Republican Minority Leader Dirksen and Republican Whip Kuchel managed to break loose a few vital votes from the long-standing Republican-southern coalition; the Johnson-Humphrey team worked one or two similar wonders on the Democratic side. The bill passed only a few weeks before the Democratic convention, and Hubert Humphrey was one of the heroes of that gathering.

With the Johnson landslide of 1964 came Democratic majorities in both houses reminiscent of New Deal days, as indicated in the following table:

Democratic Congressional Majorities, 1932–1964
(* Indicates Democratic Majority)

Year	House Democrats	Senate Democrats
1932	310*	60*
1934	319*	69*
1936	331*	76*
1938	261*	69*
1940	268*	66*
1942	218*	58*
1944	242*	56*
1946	188	45
1948	263*	54*
1950	234*	49*
1952	211	47
1954	232*	48*
1956	233*	49*
1958	283*	65*
1960	263*	64*
1962	258*	68*
1964	295*	68*

Thus, in the last seventeen Congresses, Democrats held majorities of both houses in fifteen. There was little to suggest that congressional Democrats could be dislodged from their majority status for some years to come.

CHAPTER 7

The Contemporary Presidential Party

THE OFFICE of President has expanded in responsibilities, resources, and prerogatives since the first day of the republic, often at a greater pace during wartime administrations when the President is the key figure in the military effort. The rate of growth achieved unprecedented heights, however, as the New Deal attempted to overcome the Depression crisis and as the nation struggled through World War II. If the office itself did not become something new, the partisan role of its occupants certainly did, with the help of modern mass media.

On the other hand, the congressional party was not without its development, particularly on the Senate side. Senators were for the first time popularly elected during 1913–1914. But it was probably not until the 1930's that a new generation of senatorial candidates came upon the scene with their own state electoral organizations— that is, followings distinct from or supplementary to the regular or the gubernatorial organizations. In time, senators with substantial electoral organizations of their own began to collaborate with other senators for campaign and national party purposes. Significantly, the chairmen of the Senate campaign committees became leading figures in presidential politics.

One result of the parallel growth of the partisan functions of the Presidency and the Senate has been the increased competition, already noted, between the presidential and the congressional wings.

Roosevelt's New Deal

Despite Franklin D. Roosevelt's interest in continuing his treatments for infantile paralysis at Warm Springs, New York Democrats drafted him for the governorship. Smith, as presidential nominee in 1928, fell over one hundred thousand votes behind Hoover in New York, but Roosevelt won the governorship by twenty-five thousand. When Smith announced his retirement from politics, reporters and politicians, characteristically, turned to the new Governor of New York for information about his presidential plans.

As the party faced its minority status under a Republican administration, National Chairman Raskob, with Smith's endorsement proceeded to set up a full-time national headquarters with a permanent staff headed by Jouett Shouse of Kansas City. Shouse in turn appointed Charles Michelson, a well-known newspaperman, as director of publicity. Michelson proceeded to bombard the country with anti-Hoover speeches, literature, and cartoons. In Michelson's hands the Depression could never have been caused by anything but Hoover.

Reelected governor in 1930, Roosevelt began to gather around himself a group of men whose individual and combined skills became legend: Louis M. Howe, James A. Farley, Frank C. Walker, Samuel I. Rosenman, and others. Important allies appeared in other quarters, particularly in the persons of Senators Cordell Hull, Harry Byrd, and Joseph T. Robinson, the 1928 vice-presidential nominee.

During 1931 it became increasingly evident that National Chairman Raskob was hoping to revive the Smith candidacy by his activities at national headquarters. Hull, with Farley sitting at his side, led the anti-Raskob forces, and Raskob backed away from a showdown at the annual national committee meeting. Early in 1932, Roosevelt announced his candidacy and promptly became the front-runner.

The national convention turned into a fight between two old friends: Roosevelt and Smith. A third candidate was John Nance Garner, favorite son of the Texas and California delegations. Heading the California delegation was William Gibbs McAdoo, who rose during the fourth ballot to settle old accounts with Smith. The decisive Garner votes went to Roosevelt. More than a decade had been needed to clear away the intransigence that had beset the presidential party.

The tragedy of the Depression was worldwide. The Republicans were turned out by a margin of seven million votes. Roosevelt proclaimed assuringly in his inaugural address that "the only thing we have to fear is fear itself." Congress was called into special session. A "New Deal" was in progress. And so was the inevitable internecine pushing and pulling that comes with large-scale spending programs.

Direct relief for the starving and the destitute was handled through a new Federal Emergency Relief Administration; Harry L. Hopkins became its controversial administrator. With $500 million to distribute, Hopkins found himself running a patronage machine comparable to Postmaster General Farley's, whose more than seventy-five thousand presidential appointments were no small resource. Hopkins also found himself running up against Harold L. Ickes, Public Works Administrator with other billions to spend creating jobs.

By 1935, a reaction to the vast momentum of the New Deal began to appear. Poverty and unemployment were still in evidence. The business community seemed unable to accept the rapid expansion of unionism and the new constraints imposed by collective bargaining. The notion that farmers be paid subsidies for *not* producing commodities continued to have a strange ring. With Stalin, Hitler, and Mussolini rushing to power, the strong thrust of Roosevelt's leadership frightened some who believed it might carry with it the seeds of dictatorship. Mobilizing this reaction was former Democratic National Chairman Raskob, who, with the endorsement of John W. Davis and Alfred E. Smith, inaugurated the American Liberty League. The public soon recognized that the League was a millionaires' club, and the League, in the last analysis, had little impact upon 1936 party developments.

Perhaps the only issue before the 1936 national convention was the abrogation of the two-thirds nominating rule. It was generally agreed within the party that this rule, permitting a minority to veto an otherwise popular nomination, had created all too many costly factional contests. Serious discussion regarding its abrogation began soon after the 103-ballot disaster of 1924. In the interest of harmony, the Smith forces set aside that discussion during 1928. A resolution at the 1932 convention, however, recommended to the succeeding convention that it consider the issue and make a change to majority rule. When the 1936 convention took up the matter, southerners objected, but to no avail. The elimination of the hundred-year-old rule proved in later years to have been a major step toward modification of the character of southern as well as presidential politics.

Despite its success, the 1936 campaign produced strains among old political friends. The President asked Eleanor Roosevelt to "look in" on the campaign management, which National Chairman Farley interpreted as evidence of lack of confidence in his efforts. Southern leaders, many of them still rankling over the loss of the two-thirds rule, wondered when an opportunity would arise to demonstrate their importance to the party.

Elsewhere, Harry Hopkins, social-worker-turned-politician, replaced the deceased Louis Howe as Roosevelt's confidant. Joseph P. Kennedy of Massachusetts published a businessman's appreciation of the New Deal in a volume called *I Am for Roosevelt*. The voters remained grateful, and in November gave Roosevelt every state in the Union except Maine and Vermont. In his second inaugural address, President Roosevelt expressed his hope that the work of the New Deal would continue, for he still saw "one third of a nation ill-housed, ill-clad, ill-nourished."

International politics worsened after 1937. Having successfully conquered Manchuria in 1931, the Japanese, in 1937, once again invaded China. In Europe, during 1938, Hitler annexed Austria and the Sudetenland region of Czechoslovakia. This was followed in 1939 by Germany's annexation of all Czechoslovakia and the conclusion of a nonaggression pact between Germany and Russia. Within days, Germany invaded Poland. Great Britain and France thereupon declared war on Germany. World War II had begun.

In presidential politics the great question became whether or not, in view of the world crisis, Roosevelt would seek a third term. If he did not, whom would he choose as a successor? Farley and Hull were frequently mentioned, but never by New Dealers. At the close of 1938, Roosevelt promoted Hopkins from Federal Relief Administrator to Secretary of Commerce, a move widely interpreted as a preparation for the succession. Confirmation was vigorously debated in the Senate. The following June, however, Hopkins began advocating a third term for Roosevelt, and the intensification of the war made this a growing possibility. Vice President Garner and Postmaster General Farley declared their opposition to a third term and announced their own availability.

Hopkins became the kingpin of the 1940 national convention. According to Hopkins, the President preferred Hull, Byrnes, or Wallace as his running mate. Both Hull and Byrnes declined, and the honor went to Wallace. Party leaders were nonetheless uneasy about the precedent-breaking third term nomination and refused to make Roosevelt's renomination unanimous until convention votes for Farley, Garner, and others inscribed that opposition on the record.

As Farley departed from the management of Roosevelt's campaigns, a departure that was made somewhat difficult by the unusual esteem and affection in which he was held by the party rank-and-file, a new group of men moved into the President's political staff. Hopkins, resigning as Secretary of Commerce because of ill health, worked with Rosenman and playwright Robert E. Sherwood on the president's speech-writing team. Ed Flynn took over the national chairmanship, after Joseph P. Kennedy declined.

Roosevelt defeated Willkie by a five-million-vote margin and enjoyed referring to the outcome as "close." The war against the Axis then consumed his full attention. A month after the election, he proposed Lend-Lease arrangements for aiding the Allies. By May, 1941, he found it necessary to declare an unlimited national emergency. In August he and Churchill enunciated the Atlantic Charter. On December 7 the Japanese attacked Pearl Harbor.

On the battlefields, Douglas MacArthur and his American-Philippine troops made their classic stand at Corregidor. American supply lines stretched around the Arctic Ocean to the Soviet Union, across the South Atlantic to the British in North Africa, and to the British Isles, where General Dwight D. Eisenhower trained an allied force for an invasion of the Continent.

By 1944 the Allies were able to embark upon attacks against the German lines in Italy, a new offensive in Russia, and an invasion of France. In the Pacific, MacArthur returned, as promised, to the Philippines.

The strain of the war effort took its toll upon the President who, late in 1943, began to show evidence of ill health. His renomination for a fourth term was generally accepted as fact within the party. Of greater concern to Democratic leaders was the vice-presidential nomination. Southerners would have none of Vice-President Wallace, whose radical New Dealism and statements on the race issue particularly offended them. Others available were Speaker Sam Rayburn, Senate Majority Leader Alben Barkley, Justice William O. Douglas, "Assistant President" Byrnes, and Senator Harry S. Truman, whose investigations of the defense program had given him national prominence.

Roosevelt decided to placate the southerners by putting Wallace's candidacy on its own defense. The other most active candidate was Byrnes, but his strong southern views on race soon ended his prospects. In fact, the only name without substantial political liabilities was Truman's. The President encouraged the development of circumstances that actually turned the convention to the Senator from Missouri.

Truman's Fair Deal

In his eighty-two days of service as Vice-President, Truman's major assignment was to shepherd the nomination of Henry Wallace as Secretary of Commerce through the Senate. As presiding officer of that body, Truman had to break two ties to obtain the confirmation.

On April 12, 1945, President Roosevelt's death placed the nation's principal political assignment into the hands of a man who was still widely referred to as "just an average American." To Truman were left the tasks of carrying the nation to a victorious conclusion of the global war, building the foundations of a world organization capable of guaranteeing the peace, reconverting the nation from a highly controlled war effort to a free and stable peacetime economy. After a dozen years under the leadership of the cultured patrician of Hyde Park, the American people were about to experience an entirely new brand of presidential leadership.

National and bipartisan sympathy for Truman's overwhelming burden lasted until the country was safely out of the war. The Germans agreed to unconditional surrender a month after Truman assumed the Presidency. In July, Truman, Churchill, and Stalin met at Potsdam to coordinate Pacific strategy and set the foundations for peace negotiations. As the conference proceeded, a British election put Laborite Clement Attlee at the conference table in Churchill's place. At Potsdam, Truman received word about the first successful detonation of an atom bomb by American scientists and reached the decision to drop one on Hiroshima. That bombing took place on August 5; three days later the Soviet Union belatedly declared war against Japan. The following month the Japanese surrendered.

At home the partisan honeymoon ended with the President's message of September 6 reaffirming Roosevelt's economic bill of rights of 1944. This message officially launched the Fair Deal. But the economic pathways of the Fair Deal were not easy to follow. Labor, particularly the miners and the railroad brotherhoods, went on strike to break the wage ceilings that had been imposed during the war. The President countered with a "draft-labor" plan that brought the labor movement down upon him. The strikes ended and the draft-labor proposal was dropped. Election of the Republican Eightieth Congress, however, brought in the Taft-Hartley Act, whose provisions labor viewed as harshly punitive. Truman's veto of Taft-Hartley failed. On the other hand, his support of the Full Employment Act was successful and pleased the labor interest.

In December of 1946 Truman appointed a Committee on Civil Rights to investigate the deepening problems in that field. Senators Russell of Georgia and Connally of Texas, ordinarily relatively restrained politicians, were particularly vocal in opposition to the committee. Its inevitably controversial report was rendered in October, 1947. Three months later the President sent a bill to Congress mplementing many of its recommendations. Thus, the civil rights issue became a distinguishing feature of the Truman Administration.

Truman's positions in the civil rights and the labor fields provided the broad setting of presidential politics in 1948. In response to the President's civil rights bill, a conference of southern governors sent a delegation, headed by Governor J. Strom Thurmond of South Carolina, to present their demands in Washington. In a public manifesto, over fifty southern Democrats in the House condemned the Truman civil rights program. Early in 1948, a group of southern governors revealed plans to deprive the President of their states' Electoral College vote should he become the party's nominee. The struggle went on into the national convention and the election, as we shall see.

In international affairs, President Truman led the nation in one of the most painful about-faces in its history. The nation had been a chronic disarmer, after each war embarking upon an orgy of demobilization and withdrawal of armed forces from overseas. The usual pattern appeared immediately after cessation of World War II. Fair Deal leaders, however, soon read a new handwriting on the walls of international politics.

In the wake of wartime devastation, Communist parties were making substantial electoral gains in many countries. The Soviet Union initiated tactics aimed at breaking out of the so-called capitalist encirclement. The infant United Nations seemed likely to need a powerful protector for some years. Perhaps the most unprecedented aspect of American postwar military policy was its possession of an unprecedented weapon, the atomic bomb. The bomb could hardly be used in most peacetime military operations, yet it was considered the major deterrent to Soviet aggression and a symbol of American military responsibilities around the world. These developments produced such policy issues in presidential politics as Communists-in-government; containment; support for the U.N.; the Baruch and other nuclear policy plans.

Under these circumstances, the Truman Administration slowed demobilization to a halt. In March, 1947, aid was sent to Greece and Turkey and the Truman Doctrine came into being, and with it the policy of "containment" of world communism. A few months later the Marshall Plan was launched.

The Soviet Union nonetheless held eastern Europe tightly in the grip of its occupation forces. The Chinese Communists continued to drive the Nationalists off the mainland and onto Formosa. Evidence of active Communist espionage in the United States prompted the President to request $29 million for loyalty investigations of federal employees, a move that soon led, ironically enough, to an era of Republican witch-hunting in government.

All spring and summer of 1948, the nation's organized interest groups and party factions were in turbulent disarray, trying to understand their respective places in postwar events and seeking out the political alliances that were likely to fix their commitments throughout the postwar generation. As subsequent developments suggest, probably only President Truman kept an accurate scoreboard.

Noting the resignation of General Dwight D. Eisenhower as Army Chief of Staff in February, 1948, to become president of Columbia University, Senator Russell of Georgia suggested that the hero of World War II be given the Democratic presidential nomination. Elsewhere, the Palestine crisis and the civil rights controversy, with all their implications for Jewish and Negro voters, sent Jacob R. Arvey, chairman of the Cook County organization, Mayor William O'Dwyer of New York, Leon Henderson of Americans for Democratic Action, a new anti-Communist liberal organization, and Representative James Roosevelt of California into a "dump-Truman" movement. That politics makes strange bedfellows was never more obvious.

Discouraged by the General, the Eisenhower movement never got off the ground. But other movements did. Dixiecrat forces began to take resolute steps in several southern states. Laws were changed in Virginia, Mississippi, Louisiana, South Carolina, and Alabama so that neither Truman's name nor the national party's regular symbol could appear on the ballot in the usual manner in these states. On May 10, a conference of southerners met in Jackson, Mississippi, and resolved to hold a separate national convention if Truman were nominated. Elsewhere, the strategy of the southern "regulars" was to unite behind Senator Russell as a sectional favorite son at the 1948 Democratic convention.

Another defection was under way. In 1946, although Secretary of Commerce, Henry Wallace began to enunciate foreign policy statements urging close friendship with the Soviet Union. Not only did these speeches embarrass Secretary of State Byrnes' peace treaty negotiations, they also raised doubts about the nature of Truman's "containment" policies. In September, 1946, President Truman dismissed Wallace.

New Deal liberals floundered in confusion over these developments; Wallace was a hero of that wing of the party. Meanwhile, the

Progressive Citizens of America was organized as the first phase of a movement to create the Progressive Party and nominate Wallace for President. As the extreme leftist character of the Progressive leadership became evident, New Deal liberals decided to clear the political atmosphere by establishing their own organization, Americans for Democratic Action (ADA). ADA leaders readied themselves for battles against southerners in the national convention and against Progressives in the election.

Northern liberals in the convention, following a strategy developed by the leaders of ADA, produced a minority report in the credentials committee, demanding that the Mississippi delegation be denied its seats. Incorporated in the credentials of the Mississippi delegation was a provision forbidding its delegates to bind the Mississippi party to the support of any nominee favoring Truman's civil rights program. The liberals argued that no national party could afford such dubious loyalty. Their minority report lost in a voice vote. In order to make clear the substantial size of the minority, several delegations asked the chair to put them on record in favor of the minority report. Thus, 503 votes were registered, with 618 constituting a convention majority.

The southerners, a minority in the rules committee, noting the division in the convention and hopeful of denying the nomination to Truman, proposed reinstatement of the two-thirds nominating rule. The time seemed right to them for a resurgence of southern influence in the presidential party. The proposal, however, was rejected by voice vote.

The next test came in connection with the civil rights plank. The platform committee's majority had written a relatively moderate plank. Southerners in the committee prepared three separate minority reports, each designed to water down the plank. From the convention floor, however, northern liberals, led by Mayor Hubert H. Humphrey of Minneapolis and Representative Andrew J. Biemiller of Wisconsin, offered a stronger pro–civil rights plank than any of the others. In it the Truman program was specifically endorsed. Humphrey's dramatic speech and skillful handling of floor tactics assured him a lasting place in national party affairs. The Humphrey-Biemiller plank passed, 651½ to 582½, clear evidence of a Truman majority. The Alabama delegation withdrew, and the Mississippi delegation refused to vote on the nomination. Truman was nominated with 926 votes to Russell's 266.

Probably the greatest hurdle facing the Truman campaign was

the reports of the public opinion polls, indicating that Governor Thomas E. Dewey, the Republican nominee, had approximately a 49–44 per cent lead. Democratic party workers across the nation went about their duties with grim fatalism. Meanwhile, the Dewey campaign was calm and ambiguous, designed to alienate none of the support the Governor apparently had in the bag.

In many ways, the situation was ideal for a Truman-type treatment. The President was accustomed to an underdog role. He was thoroughly familiar with the moving mosaic of national group politics that had been complicating his entire Administration. He decided to address his principal appeals to four audiences: labor, farmer, Negro, and consumer.

With the Red issue now pinned on the Wallace Progressives, organized labor could respond to the challenge of the Taft-Hartley legislation without inhibition, and in this they fervently supported Truman. If Negroes were dubious about the sincerity of Truman's civil rights policy, all doubt disappeared as a consequence of the national convention action and the bolt of the Dixiecrats. The President had wrestled with the Eightieth Congress over support of farm prices and resistance to the rising cost-of-living index and was clearly able to blame that Republican Congress for inaction in these areas. Farmers were particularly angered by declining farm prices. Perhaps most important of all was the effect of Truman's hard-hitting campaign style upon party workers; win or lose, Harry was making "the good fight," they said.

Despite Dixiecrat and Progressive defections and contrary to the forecasts of the polls, Truman came in two million votes ahead of Dewey.

Communism, Korea, and McCarthyism

American political leaders and press were increasingly absorbed by the nation's titanic confrontation with world communism. The Soviet Union sealed off occupied Berlin; the United States responded in the midst of a presidential campaign year with the Berlin airlift. The United States and eleven European nations established the North Atlantic Treaty Organization (NATO), with the American taxpayer carrying the main fiscal burden. In Asia the Chinese Communists were chasing the Chiang Kai-shek regime across the Straits of Formosa, leading to Republican charges that the Truman Administration had "lost China." In the fall of 1949 the Soviet Union detonated its irst atom bomb, and the nuclear arms race became a party issue. Things seemed to be going against the United States, and some Americans had the impression that Communists were closing in from every side.

When the Coplin and Hiss espionage cases crowded into the headlines, it seemed to some that the Communists were advancing most rapidly from inside. Coplin had been an employee of the Department of Justice and Hiss a former official of the Department of State. Hiss was found guilty of committing perjury in connection with the espionage charges against him. This trial outcome in January, 1950, paved the way for charges by Republican Senator Joseph R. McCarthy of Wisconsin the following month that the federal bureaucracy was peppered with espionage agents. In fact, said McCarthy, he knew of 205 Communists in the State Department alone. Democratic leaders, he inferred, must be either dupes or themselves co-conspirators. Thus began a spy hunt that wove in and out of a decade's election campaigning, produced nary a spy, and ended with censure of McCarthy by his colleagues in the Senate.

The Korean situation fueled the McCarthy assault upon the Democratic Party. That republic was little over a year old. Its first election had been supervised by the United Nations. American troops, stationed there alongside Soviet troops since the end of World War II, began to withdraw. Suddenly, in June of 1950, Communist North Koreans invaded the Republic of South Korea. The Communists were on the march again. President Truman ordered American military aid to the United Nations police action in Korea. McCarthy's investigations and America's fluctuating fortunes in Korea held the headlines on into the 1952 presidential year.

Southern Democrats once again decided upon Senator Russell's candidacy as a sectional instrument and in the belief that the President would not seek reelection. From another direction came announcement of the candidacy of Senator Estes Kefauver, whose crime investigations had projected him into the presidential picture. To the surprise of all, Kefauver received more votes than Truman in the early New Hampshire primary. Even though the President had not campaigned there, his political stock dropped substantially.

Although the new Twenty-second Amendment making the Presidency a two-term office technically did not prevent him from running again, the President decided he would not do so. His search for a successor took him to Governor Adlai E. Stevenson of Illinois, grandson of Cleveland's Vice-President, successful governor of a pivotal state, moderate liberal, and a distinguished representative of the United States at the United Nations. Stevenson shied away from the honor with an almost infinitive variety of imprecise phraseology.

Stevenson's ambivalence was quite real. His chance for reelection as governor of Illinois was excellent; the chance for any Democrat's election to the Presidency was, at best, fifty-fifty against a military hero of "Ike" Eisenhower's stature, and probably less. A designer of his own programs in Illinois, Stevenson's personal record would show better in a state race; but in presidential politics, it would be another man's that he would inevitably have to defend.

To further compound his perplexity, Stevenson appreciated the difficulties confronting the Democratic convention. There the Russell and Kefauver forces were bound to stalemate each other. The candidacy of the elderly Alben Barkley, beloved though he was, had all of the earmarks of a caretakership. Northern liberals, again led by ADA, were working for the imposition of a "loyalty pledge" by the convention in order to prevent the seating of disloyal Dixiecrats. With the Democratic house so divided, Stevenson appeared to be the only man close enough to the center to reunite it. At the very last minute, he agreed to allow his name to go into nomination; on the third ballot he received it.

Not since the Taft nomination in 1908 had a titular leader in the White House presented any complication in the campaign strategies of his successor. Wilson was ill during the Cox campaign in 1920, and taciturn Coolidge said little for Hoover in 1928. How could Stevenson give the party a "new look" without affronting President Truman? Stevenson's first decision was to replace National Chairman Frank McKinney, a Truman appointee and a professional politician, with Stephen A. Mitchell, a "clean amateur." This move caused endless wrangling over the organizing of the campaign. Stevenson's second decision, one rooted in his deep intellectual commitment to the educational aspects of American campaigning, was to present to the people an extensive reformulation of the "basic issues of our times."

While the Eisenhower and Taft forces were coming together on the Republican side, Democrats were running their separate ways. Stevenson set up personal headquarters in Illinois and left national headquarters in Washington to Chairman Mitchell. President Truman set out on his own whistle-stop tour, one that inevitably blurred the candidate image of Stevenson. Certain southern Democratic leaders, feeling far more comfortable with the Eisenhower-Nixon ticket, were slow in endorsing Stevenson-Sparkman. In the election, Virginia, Texas, and Florida went Republican.

Where Sits the Loyal Opposition?

The Eisenhower period was a time of particular frustration for the presidential wing of the Democratic Party. There were all the structural difficulties of out-party titular leadership: a defeated presidential nominee holding no public office (Stevenson); a former President, retired but still outspoken (Truman); a congressional leadership, after 1954, in control of both houses and protective of its prerogatives (Rayburn and Johnson); and no legitimate rostrum from which a titular leader could speak.

Stevenson and Chairman Mitchell turned to fund raising to pay off 1952 campaign debts and to prepare for the upcoming midterm election. National Committeeman Paul M. Butler of Indiana proposed a midterm national convention to help in the 1954 campaign and to perfect the presidential party machinery for the 1956 contest. Meanwhile, Stevenson addressed Democratic functions and consulted at various intervals with his "Finletter Group," an *ad hoc* "seminar" of economists, lawyers, and other Democratic public policy specialists.

When the Johnson-Rayburn leadership in 1954 assumed control on Capitol Hill, Chairman Mitchell retired to his law practice. After a knock-down national committee contest, National Committeeman Butler was elected to the chairmanship.

Butler assumed the duties with substantial energy. He began to urge upon the leaders of the congressional party that they develop a distinctively Democratic program on most issues. Stevenson and Butler were eager to formalize the activities of the Finletter "seminar" as a vehicle for broad communication within the party. Lyndon B. Johnson and Sam Rayburn, however, were reluctant to share the party stage.

In July, 1955, Senator Johnson suffered a heart attack. His name, frequently mentioned for the 1956 presidential nomination, fell from that roster. Stevenson paid his respects in a visit to the Johnson ranch in Texas during the Senator's convalescence. Speaker Rayburn also participated. Shortly after, Stevenson gathered his staff for an announcement of his candidacy. As he did, President Eisenhower suffered a heart attack. The "market value" of the Democratic nomination experienced a substantial inflation, and Stevenson found himself suddenly sharing the Democratic limelight with Senator Kefauver,

Governor Averell Harriman of New York, Governor G. Mennen Williams of Michigan, and Senator Hubert H. Humphrey. He now had to campaign hard for a nomination that he expected to be his by default.

Once renominated, and over the objections of Rayburn, Johnson, and Butler, Stevenson threw the vice-presidential choice to the open convention, and a many-sided contest resulted, which included Senator Kefauver, his junior colleague from Tennessee Albert Gore, Hubert H. Humphrey of Minnesota, and John F. Kennedy of Massachusetts.

Kefauver, Humphrey, and Kennedy were particularly well known to the delegates. Kefauver had caused the party regulars no small aggravation with his hard-hitting pre-convention campaigns in 1952 and 1956. Humphrey was an established leader of the liberal wing in the Senate and, together with former Governor Battle of Virginia, had been responsible for the skillful handling of the party's loyalty pledge problems. Kennedy, coming out of one of Massachusetts' best-known political families, had had a dramatic career and was quite conspicuous in this convention, placing Stevenson in nomination and narrating a documentary film viewed by the delegates. Kennedy also had the active backing of Majority Leader Johnson.

The vice-presidential balloting, one of the most exciting in convention history, was filled with surprises. The greatest surprise was the distribution of Kennedy's support: Georgia, Louisiana, and Virginia joining Massachusetts in support of a Catholic Democrat. Southern support was widely credited to Senator Johnson's efforts.

The second ballot was a horse race. With 686½ votes needed to nominate, Kennedy had reached 618 and Kefauver 551½. Speaker Rayburn, as permanent chairman of the convention, began to recognize delegations signaling to shift votes. With all of the skill acquired in years of leadership of the House of Representatives, Rayburn recognized a pattern of delegations that gave the prize to Kefauver, with Kennedy very close behind.

However, the unexpected achievement of Johnson's candidate was not to be forgotten. It was later speculated that Rayburn and Johnson were clearing the decks for the promotion of a fresh leadership during the inevitable second Eisenhower term.

President Eisenhower's recovery, renomination, and continued popularity added an ironic twist to the Stevenson career. The nomination Stevenson had fought so hard to obtain could again be his by default. With election odds against him, Stevenson decided once again to try to educate the electorate on the issues of the day. His most striking effort came when he called for an end to nuclear weapon testing by the major powers. This pronouncement broke a fundamental rule of American politics: never introduce an entirely new issue into the midst of a campaign.

On election day Stevenson joined William Jennings Bryan in the dubious honor of being a two-time Democratic presidential loser. Within the month, Chairman Butler brought out plans for creating a coordinating committee capable of bringing party leaders from the Senate, the House, state houses, city halls, state organizations, national headquarters, and private life into consultation with each other.

Upon his recommendation, the executive committee of the national committee authorized him to appoint a board of not more than seventeen senior Democrats who would "advance efforts in behalf of Democratic programs and principles." Butler invited some twenty leaders, including Stevenson, Truman, Mrs. Roosevelt, Speaker Rayburn, and Senator Johnson. There were eight acceptances in hand at the time he announced the invitations: Truman, Stevenson, Governor Harriman, Governor Williams, Senator Kefauver, Senator Humphrey, Mayor Tucker, and Congresswoman Green. The congressional leaders remained aloof.

On December 9, Speaker Rayburn wired Butler from Texas that he had consulted with House leaders McCormack, Albert, and Kirwan. He had concluded that it would be "a mistake" to take a place on a noncongressional policy-making body. The Speaker felt that the 233 party members in the House would probably resent their four leaders developing legislative policies on any committee outside the House.

Majority Leader Johnson also declined a few days later, noting that "legislative processes are already very difficult, and the necessity of dealing with an additional committee not created by Federal law before taking action would only cause delays and confusion." Both Rayburn and Johnson expressed their willingness to consult informally with the new Advisory Council.

The Advisory Council went it alone as an organ of the national committee. It chose a five-man steering committee, of which Stevenson was chairman. It selected a staff and established "task force" committees in each public policy field. Before the end of 1957 the Advisory Council issued some twenty-three statements on national policy. In February, 1958, as members of Congress gathered for the new session, the Advisory Council issued its own "State of the Union

Message," something of a precedent in opposition technique in the United States.

The midterm election of 1958 produced Democratic majorities of landslide proportions in both houses. In the Senate, Democratic presidential aspirants warmed up actively. Symington, Kennedy, and Humphrey put on able legislative performances, but Johnson always appeared onstage in time to take bows with each. Stevenson, however, was never entirely out of sight, even though congressional leaders rarely took public cognizance of him. In public opinion polls throughout 1958 and 1959 Stevenson ran neck-and-neck with Kennedy as the preference of Democratic voters; Johnson consistently came in third.

Despite the encouragement of Mrs. Roosevelt and other party notables, Stevenson refused to become an active candidate. Johnson's support was spread widely across the congressional ranks. Kennedy, with his youth and religion being counted as handicaps, had the most difficult demonstration to make, and this he did through one of the most aggressive and successful pre-convention campaigns in party history.

Kennedy carried the Wisconsin primary, but that contest had overtones of a Catholic-Protestant split. In the West Virginia primary, Kennedy set the religious issue straight, carrying that overwhelmingly Protestant electorate and compelling Humphrey to withdraw from the race. Thereafter, the Kennedy organization toppled one primary after the other, carrying with it decisive commitments from big-city Democratic leaders in the East and Midwest. As convention time arrived, Kennedy and Johnson forces were firing heavy ammunition at each other—but making no mention of Stevenson.

At the convention, however, a Stevenson headquarters operated with as much energy and resourcefulness as their counterparts. If Kennedy could be stopped where he was, just 160 votes short of the nomination, the prize might pass on the third or fourth ballot to either Stevenson or Johnson. For the Kennedy people, it was a first ballot nomination or bust; and first ballot nomination it became.

In a move as logical as it was traditional, Kennedy offered the second place on the ticket to his occasional mentor and major adversary, Majority Leader Johnson.

The campaign against Vice-President Nixon was never a sure thing. The public opinion polls gave each man a 52–53 per cent lead at different moments during summer and fall. The dramatic innovation of televised debates between the nominees was of mooted consequence. The press and pundits scored each man on performance; few were able to measure the precise impact on the voting outcome. Popular viewing of the debates dropped off substantially after the first round, but the first round was enough to bring the Kennedy name, face, and style abreast of the much better-known Vice-President.

New Frontiers to the Great Society

Kennedy won the election by 100,000 votes in more than 68 million cast. It was one of the closest outcomes in presidential history and one of the most evenly contested in each of the fifty states. Significantly, Nixon did as well or better than Eisenhower in six southern states. In many areas Kennedy ran behind the Democratic congressional ticket. The returns had an important bearing upon Kennedy's subsequent relations with Congress.

The nation's youngest President and his youthful entourage had hardly taken their places on the "New Frontier" before one international crisis followed another to test their mettle. As violence erupted in the Congo, Kennedy sent American support for United Nations efforts to put down the secessionist movement. As Communists poised for a take-over in Laos, Kennedy intervened to produce a fourteen-nation conference; he departed only after that country established a coalition cabinet and an uneasy truce among its factions.

Somewhat hesitantly, Kennedy endorsed long-standing plans for American support of a Cuban invasion by anti-Castro exiles, only to see that enterprise end in the Bay of Pigs debacle. In Berlin the Kennedy Administration watched as the Communists erected the Berlin Wall, and then the President used it as a symbol of the fundamental difference between freedom and totalitarianism. In the somewhat ambiguous Vietnam situation, the President increased the amount of American aid to the forces fighting the Communist Viet Cong.

The severest test came in October, 1962, at the height of the mid-term election campaign. Although it had been known for some time that the Soviet Union was increasing its supply of weapons and military advisers to Castro, it was not clear that nuclear missiles were also being shipped in. Such weaponry, universally classified as "offensive" types, at the borders of the United States represented a challenge that could not be ignored. President Kennedy placed that island under naval "quarantine" and demanded that the Soviet Union withdraw the missiles at once. This the Soviet Union eventually did, and Soviet-American relations improved appreciably thereafter.

At home, events, particularly in race relations, moved swiftly. The President's brother, Attorney General Robert F. Kennedy, gave energetic attention to the problems of Negro registration in the South. The Kennedys, with the help of Negro leaders across the country, pressed for local action in the school desegregation field as well. The Kennedy Civil Rights Bill was at the center of national and congressional attention when the President's life was taken by an assassin.

Less than two hours later, Vice-President Johnson was sworn in. Less than a week later he made clear his endorsement of the Kennedy legislative program, giving tax reduction and civil rights legislation highest priority. The tax reduction passed. So did civil rights legislation, but not without a record seventy-five-day southern filibuster. In charge of the legislation was Hubert Humphrey, the Democratic Whip, whose leadership in the national civil rights field dated back to 1948. The legislation set the stage for a conclusive reconstruction of the Democratic Party in the South.

Choosing a 1964 partner was apparently an easy personal decision for the President, for he had known and worked with Humphrey for many years. Humphrey was a northern liberal who had won the respect and trust of many southern leaders as an honorable and skillful battler for causes over which they happened to disagree. Humphrey also had a substantial following among the party rank-and-file, gathered during his previous attempts at presidential politiking in 1956 and 1960. Further, liberals and minority groups in all the major urban centers invariably warmed to the midwestern tones of Humphrey's speech. Finally, in the public opinion polls, Humphrey was first among the preferences of Democratic voters. Very close alongside, however, was Attorney General Robert F. Kennedy, the deceased President's brother.

Kennedy's political claims could not easily be disregarded. The Kennedy family name represented large achievements in national politics. It also evoked the nation's sympathy for that family's—and the nation's—recent loss. The Attorney General's handling of the many civil rights crises in the South, including the violence and murders occurring that very summer in connection with Negro voter registration drives in Mississippi, had elevated him to the status of a hero in the civil rights movement. Kennedy's youth, popular and party support, and personal resources also assured him a long and influential future in Democratic politics.

Although the war in Vietnam and the hard-nosed policies of De Gaulle in Europe offered the Johnson Administration numerous very difficult moments, the nation remained thoroughly absorbed in its domestic politics. In a tense national convention, the Republicans took a surprising turn to the right and nominated Senator Barry Goldwater and National Chairman William Miller. With the Republican prize in hand, Goldwater's subsequent behavior managed to alienate much of the eastern and some of the midwestern leadership in that party. Regardless of developments in the Republican Party, however, President Johnson's popularity in the electorate, as indicated in the public opinion polls, rarely sagged—always better than 60 per cent against any prospective Republican nominee.

Johnson's nomination was a foregone conclusion, and the 1964 national convention might easily have become a dull affair. Instead, the convention proved to be a highly professional performance, with drama and interest throughout.

The delegations from Mississippi and Alabama, ardently segregationist, were eager to stage a fight and a walkout. The groups challenging their seats were equally ardent. Humphrey worked long hours toward a compromise. At no point did he or the President lose the initiative. The compromise proposed by Humphrey would have prevented a Dixie walkout and given token recognition to the challengers, "Freedom Democrats" from Mississippi; the regular delegation would be required to sign a mild loyalty oath to support the convention's nominee. The Freedom Democrats declined; all but a handful of the Alabama and Mississippi regulars signed. Physically—that is, by convention floor seating—and strategically the President and Humphrey thoroughly isolated the southern extremists from each other, from other southerners, and from the main course of the convention.

Suspense on the vice-presidential nomination was maintained until minutes before the President arrived at Atlantic City to accept his own nomination. He then asked the delegates to choose his "trusted colleague," Hubert Humphrey.

Having resolved its major issues, the convention turned to pay respects to the deceased leader, John F. Kennedy. A commemorative film was introduced by Robert Kennedy, who received an affectionate and prolonged ovation.

Goldwater never recovered his lost Republican colleagues. However, his candidacy did push the South further along the road toward two-party competitive politics. In addition to his own state of Arizona,

Goldwater carried five southern states. The Johnson-Humphre landslide was comparable to the Roosevelt achievement in 1936. Th Electoral College outcome was 486–52. The majority status of th Democratic Party was again clearly confirmed.

The Presidential Leaders

The party in Congress is a large group, whose members and leader remain relatively anonymous or perhaps achieve a footnote in th history books. The presidential party, however, centers fairly ex plicitly around one, two, or a few men: the winning or losing pres: dential nominees; the leaders of major factions seeking to influenc the national conventions; and the national party chairmen. Historian rarely mention the names of defeated nominees and sometimes forge those of undramatic Presidents as well. In their own day, on the oth hand, Presidents and presidential nominees are among the best-know persons in the nation, and their national chairmen are often the be known of the party's "regulars." A brief examination of the mai characteristics of these men as a group may tell us much about th Democratic Party as well as about the principal leaders of its pres dential wing.

The first Democratic national nominating convention took plac in 1831. Between 1831 and 1964, inclusive, the party conducte thirty-four national conventions. These conventions have conferre the Democratic presidential nomination upon twenty-four differer men:

Jackson	Seymour	Cox
Van Buren	Greeley	Davis
Polk	Tilden	Smith
Cass	Hancock	Roosevelt
Pierce	Cleveland	Truman
Buchanan	Bryan	Stevenson
Douglas	Parker	Kennedy
McClellan	Wilson	Johnson

Two, Truman and Johnson, were elevated to the Presidency up the death of their predecessors. Many of these men have receiv little notice as national or party leaders. Only a few have, in th writer's judgment, exercised major influence upon the course of t Democratic Party generally: Jackson, Van Buren, Polk, Tilde

Cleveland, Bryan, Wilson, Roosevelt, and Truman, with the Kennedy-Johnson period too recent to evaluate.

What have *all* presidential nominees since 1831—Democratic and Republican included—been like in their social attributes, and in what attributes have Democrats differed from the norm? [1] The nominees, as a group, had the following characteristics:

1. Between the ages of fifty and fifty-four when first nominated, with Democrats closer to fifty than the Republicans.

2. Born in New York and Ohio more often than any other state, the former tending to be the principal natal state of Democrats.

3. Most often sons of professional persons, farmers, or public officials; the Democratic nominees close to the norm for the entire group.

4. Almost invariably professional persons, particularly lawyers; the Democrats much like the entire group.

5. Most have read or otherwise studied law in preparation for the bar, but they were not always holders of B.A. or LL.B. degrees; Democrats nominated the only Ph.D. (Wilson).

6. Most nominees were Presbyterians or Episcopalians, with a preponderance of Democrats in the former. Democrats are also distinguished for having placed the first member of the Catholic faith (Smith) at the head of its ticket and for having elected the first Catholic (Kennedy) to the Presidency.

7. The average presidential nominee in either major party had governmental experience in at least two or three offices, usually at the state or federal levels of government. Democrats have drawn more frequently from United States senators and state governors and less frequently than the Republicans from the military.

8. The nominees, without major differentiation between parties, have held executive positions at one or another level of the party organization.

The presidential nominee, whether he wins or loses, is only a *titular* leader of his party, under contract to run with the general support of the party. In the literal sense of a contract, the national convention *offers* him the nomination which he may or may not *accept*. He holds no formal office in the party, although he has all kinds and degrees of informal influence.

[1] The generalizations here are based on statistical analyses that include all presidential nominees from 1831 to 1956, inclusive—that is, all the Democrats mentioned—with the exception of Kennedy and Johnson, and all Whigs and Republicans up to and including Eisenhower.

If the presidential party has a *formal* leader at all, it is the national party chairman. The Democrats were the first to create this office in 1848 and have since placed thirty different men into that position:

Hallett	Jones	Flynn
McLane	Taggart	Walker
Smalley	Mack	Hannegan
Belmont (incumbent for twelve	McCombs	McGrath
years)	McCormick	Boyle
Schell	Cummings	McKinney
Hewitt	White	Mitchell
Barnum (incumbent for twelve	Hull	Butler
years and one month)	Shaver	Jackson
Brice	Raskob	Bailey
Harrity	Farley	

Democratic and Republican national chairmen, as a group, have generally had the following characteristics: [2]

1. In the forty-five to forty-nine age category at the time of first designation, with Democrats distributed along the younger side of the scale.

2. The greater number of chairmen were born in New York, Pennsylvania, or Indiana, with New York again the major source of leaders. All chairmen tended to be natives of their state of birth at the time of designation rather than transients from other states, reflecting the fact that usually they have worked their way step by step up the local, state, or national party agencies.

3. Most chairmen held either the LL.B. or a high school diploma, with Democrats tending to have slightly less formal schooling.

4. Chairmen generally had private occupations as professional persons or public officials.

5. The most numerous religious affiliation among Democratic chairmen has been the Catholic faith; Presbyterian among the Republicans.

6. The governmental experience of the chairmen was mainly in state legislatures and appointive federal posts.

In general, the presidential nominees have tended to have social

[2] These generalizations are based upon analyses that include chairmen in office between 1848 and 1959. Thus, the figures do not cover Democratic National Chairmen Jackson and Bailey.

and economic attributes as broadly diversified as those found of the American electorate at large. The national chairmen, on the other hand, have been fairly typical of the characteristics of the rank-and-file in their respective parties. The chairmen have been "organization men"—increasingly so in recent decades, and more so on the Democratic side—in that they have had many years of experience in party work and have gone up the organizational ladder steadily through their careers.

If we remember that the nation did not settle down into a stable two-party system until the post-Reconstruction era, we may understand why particular presidential party leaders were so important in the fortunes of the early national parties. In fact, with the exception of the Democratic Party, national party organizations blossomed and disintegrated with great frequency before the 1880's. Even the Democrats, without a great national military hero like Andrew Jackson, might have had some difficulty in gathering themselves and remaining so.

During the four decades between 1840 and 1880 entire factions of the two major national parties followed their leaders from one party banner to another. Particular leaders were objects of greater voter loyalty than were party names and organizations. From the 1880's to the present, however, the overwhelming majority of the voters—upward of 96 per cent—have become thoroughly accustomed to and persistently loyal to the national Democratic and Republican parties. In closely contested presidential elections, third parties and major factional defections may indeed make a great difference in a particular outcome, but are not likely to last. History will probably show that the Progressives following Theodore Roosevelt as he walked out of the Republican Party were the last of the truly major follow-our-leader movements in presidential politics. Within the contemporary two-party framework, however, the presidential party leader, individually, still enjoys great influence. Win or lose, persistent factions form around the candidacies of particular men and tend to be reluctant to disband, as in the cases of Wilson, Roosevelt, Stevenson, and others.

One discovery of recent investigations of party behavior is that the party name, as a symbol, holds the loyalties of innumerable voters whose favorable attitude arose during the party's collective responses on *past* occasions. On the other hand, popular attitudes toward the presidential party leaders as personalities and as spokesman on particular issues seem to be derived from more *recent* influences in national politics.[3] Thus, the individual presidential party leaders, their names, their personalities, their renown, all combine in one degree or another to help shape the contest between the two major presidential parties.

[3] Angus Campbell *et al., The American Voter* (New York: Wiley, 1960), p. 60.

CHAPTER 8

Emerging Tendencies and Future Dilemmas

THE DEMOCRATIC PARTY has come a long way through history, hand in hand with the nation it has governed so often and served so well. ✤In this decade, Democrats constitute a majority party at almost all levels of government. The voting margins favoring the Democrats seem substantial enough to assure a long tenure as the majority.

But no experienced politician, least of all one trained as a Democrat, rests on laurels or sleeps on the status quo, particularly in a society as dynamic as the American or a world that changes by the decade rather than by the century as of old. The future crowds upon us at an unprecedented pace, with unfamiliar problems to identify and hitherto unknown alternatives to chose from. Action in the present seems less and less tied to the past and increasingly contingent upon our pictures of the future.

What are some of the future problems that are likely to confront Democrats as a political party? The nature of some of these problems may be guessed from the evidence of recent trends. A few of these will be reviewed here. The alternatives to be chosen by the party are something else again—matters for the Democratic dialogue of decades and generations to come.

Dissolution of the Solid South

✶ Probably the most highly visible trend in Democratic Party affairs is the disappearance of the "Solid South." These were the eleven states that, between the end of Reconstruction (about 1876) and the end of the New Deal (mid-1940's), almost unanimously gave their votes to Democrats: for President; for their governors and state legislators; for United States senators and representatives; for mayor and school board members. These solidly Democratic states included Alabama, Arkansas, Florida, Georgia, Louisiana, Mississippi, North Carolina, South Carolina, Tennessee, Texas, and Virginia. The Solid

South appeared as a reaction to the conditions of the Reconstruction era.

Scarred by the battles of the Civil War, southerners sought post-war protection in the secret armies of the Ku Klux Klan. Without economic resources to replace lost slave property and ravaged lands, the South sank into economic impoverishment, with its grim companions, ignorance and extremism. Victims of the Reconstruction program of the Radical Republicans, the South in turn victimized the Republican Party, excluding it almost entirely from its precincts and its ballots.

Perhaps worst of all was the racial reaction to Reconstruction, for it focused the brunt of southern frustration and dissatisfaction upon an accessible human target: the Negro. The angry southern white found psychological release in kicking around his former slave property. The southern Negro, without group traditions to lend ego-support and fearful of migrating from the land of his childhood, accepted this treatment as part of the "natural order" of things.

What was the political hardware of post-Reconstruction southern influence in the Democratic Party and the nation? There were several key pieces of equipment.

1. Sheer legislative numbers. Nearly a fourth of all the seats in Congress have been occupied by senators and representatives from these eleven states.

2. The two-thirds nominating rule. Prior to 1940, Democratic national conventions required a two-thirds majority to nominate. With unity among themselves and a few additional votes from border states or splinter factions, the southerners learned how to veto any candidate who failed to lend a proper ear to their demands.

3. The filibuster. The United States Senate permits unlimited debate, assurance that any protest or dissent worthy of at least one—not to mention twenty-two—senator's interest will be articulated, heard, and perhaps even bring the legislative process to a standstill.

4. The white primary. By poll taxes, special literacy requirements, grandfather clauses, and other election administration devices, southern whites were able for decades to exclude Negroes almost entirely from the electoral process, leaving the selection of public officers and policies to local "machines."

5. Seniority. In Congress, long tenure produced seniority, and seniority led to committee chairmanships and other powerful posts. A Democratic majority in either house of Congress put a phalanx of southerners at most of the major gateways of legislation.

6. The race issue. When no other clarion call for unity worked, the southern politician always had the race issue to fall back upon.

What happened to these pieces of political equipment in recent decades? They began to tarnish, decay, and disappear.

1. The New Deal and Great Society landslides gave the Democrats legislative majorities that could produce decisions with or without votes from southern legislators.

2. One hundred years of the two-thirds nominating rule ended in 1936, in part as a result of southern abuse of that rule in the stalemated conventions of 1920 (44 ballots) and 1924 (103 ballots).

3. The use of the filibuster was modified, only slightly, by a 1917 cloture procedure requiring a two-thirds vote of those present and voting. In 1949, and regularly thereafter, the Senate has seen renewed efforts to broaden the cloture provisions.

4. The white primary has been under attack in the courts since the 1920's. The Classic (1941), Allwright (1944), and other decisions by the Supreme Court have placed constraints upon this practice. The Civil Right Acts of 1957, 1960, and 1964 armed the Attorney General with additional powers. Negro registration in the South has risen from 1,008,614 in 1952 to 2,164,200 in 1964.

5. Congressional seniority, particularly in the Senate, has been subject to dilution for almost a generation. In addition to party affiliation and seniority, committee assignments now take into account geographical location, special competence, factional attachment, and other factors. The "Johnson rule" of the Eighty-third Congress added still another diluent: each new Democratic member of the Senate is to receive at least one major committee assignment.

6. The race issue, ostensibly the most stubborn of all, may in fact disappear more rapidly than some of the others. Race as one factor in intergroup and interpersonal relations will of course remain, as do religion, nationality, educational achievement, occupational training, income, and a host of other factors that differentiate human beings one from the other. Race as a *political* issue, however, is expendable, and for the new generation of southern politicians, its reiteration could be costly. It is sheer political suicide to kick the hand that may drop a vote against you into the ballot box.

What problems do these trends create for the Democratic Party? Several come to this writer's mind.

Southerners, as old hands in national politics, are not likely to remain outmaneuvered for long in Congress, and are quite likely to find new grounds for sectional collaboration, possibly with Democrats in the West and Southwest.

The end of the two-thirds rule is likely to produce a bifactional, as has been the tendency in the Republican Party, rather than a multifactional party.

Cloture is likely to remain, for it reflects a profound American concern for the protection of minority rights, legislative minorities as well as racial.

Millions of Negro citizens have yet to be registered and enabled to vote.

Possibly the most uncertain of the difficulties concerns the retraining of the present Democratic leadership in the South and the recruitment of new ones. Some contemporary southern leaders seem, like Strom Thurmond, to have a happier home among the Republicans; other defections will undoubtedly occur. Other contemporary southern leaders, like Richard Russell, have been "fixed in the mold" for very long and are not amenable to change. Still others, like Russell Long, seem willing to cope directly with the volatile new conditions, facing the inescapable risk of moving too fast or too slowly or failing altogether.

Will the new leaders be prepared to deal with a highly competitive politics? Will they be ready to cope with an era of rapid economic and social growth in the South, which, while catching up with the rest of the nation in every area of human endeavor, will be changing at a more accelerated pace than the rest of the nation?

Expanding Competition for the Electorate

The dissolution of the one-party South has been accompanied by a decline in one-party Republican areas as well. A Democratic senator is elected in Maine. A Democratic governor is elected in Vermont. The Republican Midwest is contested territory. These are as remarkable, from the point of view of the history of political competition, as Georgia, South Carolina, Mississippi, Alabama, and Louisiana voting for a Republican presidential nominee. From the race for President to those for local commissioner, the American voters are dividing more evenly and remaining less attached to the two major parties. The growing competition is the cumulation of long-run trends and is likely to produce narrower victories all up and down the ballot.

There are several ways of measuring the degree of competitiveness etween parties. The simplest is to observe if control of public offices hanges party from election to election; high turnover means much ompetition. Another method, more sensitive, is to measure the elative closeness of voter support for the two major parties.

This can be done by producing "Stalemate Indexes" for each set f election returns.[1] The following table compares the Indexes for 952, 1956, 1960, and 1964. (The Indexes with a minus sign indicate at the Republicans carried the state.)

State Stalemate Indexes in Recent Presidential Voting

tate	1952	1956	1960	1964	1952–1964 Average	1952–1964 Standard Deviation
labama	14.8	8.6	7.5	−14.3	4.1	11.0
laska	0.0	0.0	−0.9	15.9	3.7	7.0
rizona	−8.3	−11.0	−5.6	−0.3	−5.0	2.9
rkansas	6.1	3.3	3.6	6.3	4.8	1.4
alifornia	−6.8	−5.6	−0.3	9.2	−0.9	6.3
olorado	−10.7	−9.9	−4.9	11.5	−3.5	9.0
onnecticut	−5.9	−13.7	3.7	17.9	0.5	11.8
elaware	−1.9	−5.2	0.8	11.1	1.2	6.1
lorida	−5.0	−7.3	−1.5	1.1	−3.2	3.2
eorgia	19.7	16.6	12.6	−4.1	11.2	9.2
awaii	0.0	0.0	0.0	28.8	7.2	12.4
laho	−15.5	−11.2	−3.8	0.9	−7.4	6.4
linois	−4.9	−9.6	0.1	9.5	−1.3	7.1
ndiana	−8.6	−10.1	−5.2	6.2	−4.4	6.4
)wa	−14.1	−9.2	−6.7	12.0	−4.5	9.9
ansas	−19.1	−15.6	−10.7	4.5	−10.2	9.0
entucky	0.0	−4.5	−3.6	14.2	1.5	7.5
ouisiana	2.9	−6.9	10.9	−6.8	0.0	7.4
laine	−16.1	−20.9	−7.0	18.8	−6.3	15.3
aryland	−5.8	−10.0	3.6	15.5	0.8	9.8
lassachusetts	−4.4	−9.5	10.3	26.4	5.7	14.0
lichigan	−5.7	−5.7	1.0	16.8	1.6	9.2
linnesota	−5.6	−3.8	0.7	13.9	1.3	7.6

[1] The "Stalemate Index" is a measure of the percentage relationship between e two leading parties as these in turn relate to the total vote cast. This Index lls us in a single figure how many percentage points the principal losing party ould have to gain in the electorate in order to tie or stalemate the winning rty. For example, New York in 1960 gave 52.5 per cent of its total vote to ennedy, 47.3 per cent to Nixon, and 0.2 per cent to others. One half the per- ntage difference between the Nixon-Kennedy votes—that is, 2.6 points—is e Stalemate Index or proportion of the electorate that Nixon would have had gain to tie Kennedy in New York.

State Stalemate Indexes in Recent Presidential Voting—Continued

State	1952	1956	1960	1964	1952–1964 Average	1952–1964 Standard Deviation
Mississippi	10.4	16.9	5.8	−37.1	−1.0	21.2
Missouri	−0.8	0.1	0.3	14.7	3.6	6.4
Montana	−9.7	−7.1	−1.3	9.2	−2.2	7.3
Nebraska	−19.2	−15.5	−12.1	2.6	−11.0	8.3
Nevada	−11.4	−8.0	1.2	8.6	−2.4	7.8
New Hampshire	−10.9	−16.1	−3.4	13.6	−4.2	11.3
New Jersey	−7.4	−15.2	0.4	15.9	−1.6	11.5
New Mexico	−5.6	−8.0	0.4	9.5	−0.9	6.7
New York	−5.9	−11.2	2.6	18.6	1.0	11.3
North Carolina	3.9	0.7	2.1	6.2	3.2	2.1
North Dakota	−21.3	−11.8	−5.4	8.0	−7.6	10.7
Ohio	−6.8	−11.1	−3.3	12.9	−2.1	9.1
Oklahoma	−4.6	−5.1	−9.0	5.7	−3.2	5.5
Oregon	−10.8	−5.2	−2.6	13.9	−2.1	9.2
Pennsylvania	−2.9	−6.6	1.2	15.1	1.7	8.2
Rhode Island	−0.9	−8.3	13.6	30.9	8.8	15.0
South Carolina	0.7	10.1	1.2	−8.9	0.8	6.7
South Dakota	−19.3	−8.4	−8.2	5.6	−7.6	8.8
Tennessee	−0.1	−0.3	−3.6	5.5	0.4	3.3
Texas	−3.2	−5.6	1.0	13.4	1.4	7.3
Utah	−8.9	−14.6	−4.8	16.9	−2.9	11.9
Vermont	−21.6	−22.2	−8.6	16.3	−9.0	15.6
Virginia	−6.5	−8.5	−2.7	3.7	−3.5	4.6
Washington	−4.8	−4.2	−1.2	12.3	0.5	6.9
West Virginia	1.9	−4.1	2.7	17.9	4.6	8.1
Wisconsin	−11.1	−11.9	−1.9	12.3	−3.1	9.7
Wyoming	−12.8	−10.1	−5.0	6.6	−5.3	7.4

As the table indicates, thirty-eight of the states have Stalemate Indexes whose 1952–1964 average is less than five points—that is, fairly competitive presidential electorates within their borders. Further, when the standard deviations of these thirty-eight states are examined, we find that thirty-five of the thirty-eight fluctuate narrowly enough within their own ranges to lead us to expect that they will remain competitive for some time to come. It is interesting to note that the least volatile electorates are those of Arkansas, North Carolina, and Arizona, whereas the most volatile are those in Maine,

Vermont, and Mississippi, old one-party states now going through periods of rapid change in voting patterns.[2]

These particular statistics tell of party competition in the presidential electorate. Similar statistics would undoubtedly produce similar findings for a growing number of constituencies at the congressional, state, and local levels of contest.

In a society where competition is a familiar and valued condition of life, problems arising from the intensification of party competition will be readily recognized:

1. Party policy positions and campaign appeals will become increasingly alike. This reflects not only the broad consensus that exists on most basic issues but also the need for both parties to appeal to the same uncommitted voters in the middle if an election majority is to be obtained. On the other hand, new and serious public issues will have to make their way into the center of the political marketplace via new minor parties or new minority factions within each of the major parties.

As in the 1880's and 1890's, these minorities will obtain a hearing only if they can be pivotal to the outcome of the major-party races. Should party and factional minorities be safeguarded and their contributions to American politics facilitated? How should these arrangements be made? The questions are likely to become compelling over the next decades.

2. A consequence of increased competition may be stalemate and indecision in some matters of public policy. An evenly divided political community may have no trouble moving ahead in policy areas where there is general agreement on fundamentals and disagreement on only minor aspects. However, what if there should be intense disagreement on the fundamental aspects of a public problem? What if the disagreement should coincide with party lines, as in 1828, 1860, 1896, and 1932, years of our most bitter presidential campaigns? Those campaigns climaxed years of stalemate and inertia in critical

---

[2] The standard deviation is a measure of the rate of departure of given data from their own mean. Thus, the 1952–1964 average Stalemate Index for Arkansas is 4.8. Its standard deviation is 1.4, indicating that in slightly over two thirds of the cases included in that mean the cases departed from the mean by 1.4 points or less.

The thirty-five out of thirty-eight states whose Stalemate Indexes fluctuated "narrowly" were those whose standard deviations were smaller than their means—that is, whose normal departures from the average were not likely to cross the stalemate line in the balance between the parties.

areas of public policy, and one was followed by civil war. If suc circumstances are likely to occur again, what institutional and oth safeguards may the nation develop to prevent the political paralys that sometimes accompanies the even division in its electorates?

3. As competition tightens, campaigning intensifies. Not unlil many American industries, the political parties, as producers an purveyors of public leaders and public policies, will be expendi more and more resources delivering their "messages" about produc that seem less and less distinguishable (see previous text). Th consequences for political campaigning may be many.

The cost of campaigns will rise not only as a result of the expei siveness of newer communication technologies such as television b simply because there will be more and bigger campaign efforts. Th time needed for campaign preparation and buildup will also becon greater, as it already has; party campaigns will become election-t election enterprises.

In view of the vital public service rendered by the parties, w public revenue resources be used to help parties meet these hig costs? How can the "equal time" principle be modified to furnis guidance in the distribution of such resources to the major parties an to the perhaps increasingly indispensable minor parties? What pos tions will the Democratic Party—itself short on money but long c organization—take on these matters?

4. Another consequence of intensified competition and more can paigning will be increased organization. As party operations becon year-round, as growing numbers of competitive districts have to l coordinated at once, and as financial and other resources have to l regularized, it will become increasingly necessary to maintain perm: nent party headquarters, full-time professional staffs, and stable lin of communication and political intelligence at all levels of par effort. In other words, it becomes inevitable that formal party o ganization will grow.

The tendency has, of course, already begun at different speeds c different levels. National party headquarters have grown in sta office space, budget, and function since they became "permanent" the late 1920's and earlier 1930's. The congressional campaign con mittees have experienced similar growth during the 1940's an 1950's, particularly as midterm contests became more numerous an demanding of coordinated effort. Finally, greater numbers of sta and local parties are trying to find means to support permanent hea quarters and regular staff. Will such means—in untarnished money and well-trained men—be found? Will the American people see party organizational growth as a threat to be constrained or a public service to be promoted?

Coordination of Congressional and Presidential Parties

Much of the historical account of this volume has been set forth as the story of the Democratic Party in Congress and the Democratic Party in the Presidency. As the reader will undoubtedly have noticed, descriptions of many of the same general political events recur in both the congressional and presidential histories. But, significantly, in each, different perspectives, leaders, and decisions come into view.

Political parties, as the managers of government, cannot avoid reflecting in their own organizational structure the structure of the governments they manage. Thus, in the United States, the Democratic and Republican parties have been as federal as the nation and as divided at the national level as the national branches of government. James MacGregor Burns has referred to this condition as "a four-party system," each of the two major national parties consisting of two distinct parties: the congressional and the presidential.[3]

While this has, organizationally and practically, been true, it has also been true that the national parties—in their respective legislative coalitions, nominating conventions, campaign collaborations, and countless techniques for informal consultation—have served as vital "connectors," to use the term of Edmund Burke and Henry Jones Ford, among men of like mind in the various separated branches and levels of government.[4]

The future of American party politics promises to thrust these "men of like mind" closer together as they face the challenge of intensified competition and enlarging organization. Thus, the congressional and presidential wings of both national parties are likely to be under greater pressure to coordinate their agencies, resources, personnel, policies, and public images. This coordination, compelling as it may be, is not likely to be easy to design and implement. The independence of party leaders in the Presidency, in the Senate, and in the House of Representatives has had important practical as well

[3] *The Deadlock of Democracy* (Englewood Cliffs: Prentice-Hall, 1963).

[4] Henry Jones Ford, *The Rise and Growth of American Politics* (New York: Macmillan, 1898), pp. 128–129, 215.

as constitutional implications. Dispersion of the units of power has permitted leaders to pull together new coalitions more in keeping with the times. A multiplicity of routes to power has given new leaders greater opportunity for rising in the system. The diverse interests of a complex society are more likely to be represented by competing leaders than by "safe" leaders who need not trouble to listen. As a result, coordination of congressional and presidential agencies and leaderships is likely to be among the more difficult problems faced by the Democratic Party.

Not that efforts at coordination have never been made! Members of Congress show up as leaders and delegates at the presidential nominating conventions, sometimes, as in 1952, serving in vital conciliatory capacities among the warring factions. In recent years, Congress, particularly the Senate, has in fact been a principal supplier of presidential timber: Truman, Kefauver, Symington, Russell, Humphrey, Kennedy, and Johnson. Presidents and presidential candidates have been increasingly available for duty as campaigners in midterm congressional elections; President Kennedy in 1962 actually provided the central impetus and coordinative mechanisms for that off-year campaign. The presidential wing, particularly during the Stevenson years, created the Democratic Advisory Council hopefully to serve as a policy-pronouncing forum among Democratic leaders in and out of Congress.

The efforts and inventions will unquestionably continue as national Democrats face the need to coordinate their congressional and presidential parties for a better battle against the opposition.

Adapting Stationary Machines for Mobile Voters

Democrats in their state and local organizations will also experience growing pains. We have, in Chapter 3, already noted some of these problems: Will procedures be devised for reconciling factional contests within the state and local party organs at the same time allowing for free expression of factional differences? Will the hub of statewide party organizations be the United States senator or the governor when the party fills either or both of these offices? As state legislative reapportionment tends to produce a modernized Republican Party over the years to come, will Democrats be recruiting and training state leaders equally skilled in the tasks of a highly competitive politics?

However, still another kind of problem will continue to beset state and local organizations. About 20 per cent of the American people currently move from one residence to another each year. In the mid-1960's this amounts to about 38,000,000 persons, including children. Of these, some 6,100,000 move from one state to another, another 5,900,000 move from one county to another, and over 25,000,000 move within the same county but probably between precincts and wards. Of the 38,000,000 movers, some 23,000,000 are adults who are potential voters. And it is the local party organization that must keep track of these mobile but potential voters every year!

Innumerable local party leaders will testify to the administrative drain that is created by the need to keep up with local arrivals and departures of resident voters. Add to this administrative chore the racial, educational, and economic concomitants of voter mobility and we have some impression of the scope of the challenge to local party leaders and organizations all across the nation.

Further, add the reduced cost of travel from one part of the nation to the other, the comprehensive coverage of events provided by the national mass media, and the willingness of citizens in one part of the country to help their fellow citizens politically in another part, and we can appreciate the growing impact of "outsiders" upon local politics. It is even becoming fashionable for party leaders in one part of the nation to take up residence and run for office in another.

One consequence of all this mobility is likely to be an end to local community political isolation. Local and state politics are not going to escape the events of nearby or, for that matter, remote communities. What happens in Selma, Alabama, has consequences for party politics in New York, Chicago, and San Francisco, and vice versa.

Another consequence is likely to be a less fixed partisan complexion in the cities. The "Democratic cities" may be less and less so. One of the great subterranean issues of urban redevelopment programs, for example, is the impact they may have upon the voting composition of the redeveloped areas. If redevelopment produces high-priced dwellings for high-income voters, Republican voters are likely to live where Democrats lived before. On the other hand, if racial and other minorities tend to flock into the cities, whole urban communities could, for a generation or two at least, become political as well as social ghettoes.

These are some of the factors about the mobile voting population that give local party leaders such as Wagner, Daley, and Shelley a

feeling of harassment that their nineteenth-century Tammany counterparts rarely experienced. And the feeling is likely to get worse.

Emergence of International Party Alliances

For one hundred years the marxists—both Communist and Socialist—have been practitioners of international political party organization and collaboration. They organized the short-lived First
International (1864–1874), the Second International (1889–1917),
Third International, or Comintern (1919–1943), and, after 1947,
the Communist Information Bureau, or Cominform.

The Communist model has been imitated by the Socialist Interna-
tional (1923) and its postwar successor, the International Socialist
Conference (1946), by the Liberal International (1947), and by the
Christian Democratic Party alliances in Europe.

In brief, national political parties in many parts of the world have
been entering into cross-national alliances and organizations in order
to facilitate the achievement of particular international political
objectives which they share: the promotion of shared policies in
international bodies such as the United Nations or the European
Parliamentary Assembly; the articulation of ideological and propaganda positions in world affairs; the influencing of constitutional
development in regional and world political institutions, such as the
United Nations or a United Europe; the capture of international
public offices, such as the presidency of the U.N. General Assembly
and of national offices as well, such as the presidency of Cuba.

But the concept of international party activity is so novel—and
perhaps even abhorrent—to most Americans that public discussion of
this approach to world politics is practically nonexistent.[5] Yet, as
the Cold War progresses along political as well as economic and
military lines, the American people—particularly their party leaders
—will be compelled more and more to face the fact that the political
party is a vital tool in world as well as national politics. Thus, for
example, in Southeast Asia the Communists have an effective alliance
system among several military organizations: the People's Army of
North Vietnam, the Viet Cong of South Vietnam, and the Pathet
Lao of Laos. But—and this is the point that most Americans miss—

[5] See this author's "The Political Context of Arms Control: A Systems
Approach," in J. David Singer (ed.), *Weapons Management in World Politics;*
special issue of *Journal of Conflict Resolution* (September, 1963).

the Communists also have an effective alliance system in Southeast Asia among *several party organizations,* quite apart from, though closely cooperating with, the military: the Communist Party of North Vietnam, the National Liberation Front of South Vietnam, the Neo Lao Hak Xat Party of Laos, and so on.

In their search for political weapons less drastic than war yet more potent than the usual devices of formal diplomacy, American party leaders—Democratic and Republican alike—will have to imitate the Communist adversary as well as our allies, by turning more and more to international party organization as a means to a variety of international objectives. What are some of the specific activities that the Democratic Party could find itself involved in were it to turn seriously, as inevitably it must, to a search for international party allies? Some of these activities could include

1. Transcending the rigidities of formal diplomacy by providing the West with a free-wheeling vehicle with which to wage psychological diplomacy against the totalitarians.

2. Unifying the "Campaign of Truth" by serving as an informational and communications clearinghouse for the democracies and by flushing into the open Communist conspiracy, subversion, and corruption wherever it occurs.

3. Providing an agency for the development of democratic political leaders at all levels and a rostrum for the world spokesmen of the democracies.

4. Pressing the ideological debate and broadening the universe of world political discourse.

5. Promoting the constitutional development of the United Nations, particularly in debates over its Charter and its functions; most immediately, probably, promoting the growth of the legislative function in the United Nations.

6. Organizing the grass roots throughout the world by establishing world party conventions and promoting collaboration among existing antitotalitarian parties.

7. Prodding the Communist top echelons into factional disagreement by discovering and magnifying differences within the Communist elite and by publicly challenging the illusion of "indomitable shrewdness" that Western observers seem so willing to attribute to Communist leaders in the Kremlin, Peking, Hanoi, and elsewhere.

American party leaders cannot long afford to overlook the realities of world party organization. The world is our precinct.

Promoting the "Profession" of Democratic Party Leadership

In the last analysis, of course, the most fundamental future problem of the Democratic Party is the adequate replenishment of its leadership resources. New operating conditions in the South, growing competition for voter support in every corner of the nation, coordination of congressional and presidential wings, difficulties of party administration at the state and local levels, representation of the Democratic voters of the future, grasp of the requirements of world party developments—these and other future problems will be meaningless without the trained and resourceful leadership manpower to understand and deal with them. If nothing else, a political party is an organization seeking to place *its leaders* into public offices and to obtain for *its leaders* certain initiatives in public policy-making. In sum, a party is naught without, and everything with, skillful leaders.

Two basic tenets in the American philosophy about politics are (1) that *any* adult individual *can* be a politician and (2) that *every* citizen *should* try to be politically active—that is, a working politician. The plain empirical facts are, however, (1) that politics is a highly specialized and demanding kind of work and (2) that most people, including Americans, are not and cannot be interested in becoming politicians.

To illustrate the first point, the nomination of John F. Kennedy and Richard M. Nixon in 1960 was considered a rare thing in American political history; of the more than three hundred persons who have been considered serious candidates for President or Vice-President, these two were among a tiny handful who had as much as fourteen years of experience in national government (as representatives, senators, and, in Nixon's case, Vice-President). The rarity was in the electorate's opportunity to have *two* such highly trained men to chose from *at the same time.*

But even the candidate for dogcatcher must have specialized political knowledge: what his prospective constituency consists of; what vote it takes to win; how to campaign and win support; how to differentiate between a campaign promise and a public policy; how to get nominated; how to raise money and other resources for campaigning and for the operation of the government; when to fight and when not to fight; and on and on.

On the second point—that most people are not interested in becoming politically active—we need only mention two facts: that nearly one third of the eligible voters fail to vote in the principal of our elections, the presidential; and that nearly two thirds fail to vote in a very substantial number of local elections. How many political activists are there in the United States? Various estimates have been offered: (1) two per cent of the adult population; (2) a few hundred in each state plus a few thousand in Washington, D.C.; (3) a million or so persons generally, including such occasional activists as poll watchers.

If not many citizens are interested in political work and if very few have acquired the highly specialized skills, who is to lead the parties and fill the offices of government? As every party leader worth his salt knows, the general supply of personnel is small indeed—and the supply of talented personnel almost infinitesimal.

Thus it is that the Democratic Party will continue to be in a seller's market for the supply of political talent. Given only a few of the trends noted earlier, the demand for professionalism in party management will increase by leaps and bounds. Given all of them, the shortage may prove onerous and debilitating.

In view of all this, the party will need to expand its few programs and invent new programs for recruiting leadership talent. The party will need to encourage political training programs in the schools and colleges. Political internships and systematic on-the-job instruction will have to be organized more seriously. Schemes will have to be designed for giving the more promising recruits a wide range of practical experience in campaign, organizational, legislative, and other areas of party work.

The Democratic Party cannot and should not try to train the philosopher-kings so ardently recommended by Plato. But the Democratic Party can and must continue to produce the high-quality professional politicians—the skilled political brokers—that have led it through a long, proud history and have elevated it to the nation's majority party today.

A Do-It-Yourself Presidential Election Forecasting Kit

Americans are inveterate score-keepers. Baseball scores, football scores, stock market reports, and, of course, election returns. Underlying all this is a cultural heritage that esteems vigorous but peaceful competition, decisive but fair play, and a pragmatic recognition that performance records tell us much about the expectations we may have for probable outcomes in future contests.

Thus, politicians and pundits begin interpreting the last election returns even before the votes are completely counted. Contending factions and prospective candidates start from the last set of votes as they build up for the next nominating contests. Party leaders study returns and opinion polls as sources of information about how and where best to direct their efforts in upcoming nomination, platform, campaign, and other party activities.

The statistical exercise below is a consequence of the author's own interest in presidential election score-keeping. However, the exercise also involves some useful propositions about the voting behavior of the electorate generally, and the presidential electorate specifically. These propositions—some of which will seem quite obvious—are as follows:

1. In its voting patterns for *particular offices* most constituencies maintain a high degree of consistency. The point emphasized here is the significance to be attached to the office being voted for. In a particular state, for example, its presidential electorate needs to be studied apart from its gubernatorial, senatorial, and other kinds of electorates. In the analysis below, we have studied the presidential electorate in each of the states, that is, the Democratic, Republican, and "other party" votes for state electors in the Electoral College.[1]

2. Because of this consistency in voting patterns, the returns from the last election normally tell us a great deal about how the parties will divide in the next election. Study of the last election is, in fact, the basis for most analyses currently made by practicing politicians. However, this one-election kind of evidence *wastes* a great deal of useful data readily available in the returns of earlier elections. A two-, three-, or four-election analysis may tell us a great deal more about the constituency's average behavior, trends, and degrees of relative volatility. Time series and trend analyses are the kinds of tools that business firms, for example, have in

[1] The District of Columbia, with its three Electoral College votes, participated for the first time in 1964 and is omitted from this analysis.

recent decades come to find indispensable for their production and sales decisions. In the analysis below, we have adopted the four-election time series; the forecast for 1964 was based upon the state returns of 1948–1960.[2]

3. In voting for particular offices, sub-constituencies—like soldiers marching to war or football players lining up on the field—tend to maintain a high degree of rank-order consistency. In other words, when voting for President, most states, as Electoral College sub-constituencies within the nation as a whole, tend to have the same neighbors on the pro-Democratic or pro-Republican side of the line-up; e.g., Ohio and Pennsylvania usually land close to each other. If the rank-orders of the states in several successive elections are studied, long-run shifts in party alignment become readily observable; e.g., Mississippi's and South Carolina's long-run shift from the Democratic end of the roster to the Republican. In the analysis below, the 1964 and 1968 rank-orders are forecasted and placed side by side.

4. There is a systematic relationship between nationwide swings in presidential preference and the way a state will vote in the Electoral College. As the informed citizen knows, the real decision on the Presidency is made in the Electoral College, whereas the Gallup Poll and other polls endeavor to predict how the voters-in-the-mass will divide proportionately. However, there has been no procedure for economically forecasting how a 65-35, a 56-44, or some other voters-in-mass division may affect the outcome in the Electoral College. In the analysis below, the procedure for finding the "Electoral College cut-off point" attempts this kind of forecast with substantial success.

Let us now examine the 1964 Electoral College Forecast below. Analyzing the 1948–1960 presidential Stalemate Indexes for each state by parabolic regression formula, the Predicted Stalemate Indexes for 1964 were found and listed in the first column.[3]

The Predicted State Stalemate Indexes were listed in rank order from 70.6 for Alabama, the most Republican on the roster, to 129.7 for Rhode Island as the most Democratic. Indexes below 100 show Republican leanings; those above 100 Democratic leanings.

Various statistical experiments by the author have confirmed that a fairly consistent relationship exists between each of these State Stalemate Indexes and the National Stalemate Index. The National Stalemate Index is simply the index derived from the nationwide, voters-in-the-mass percentage division of the presidential vote. Thus, if the nationwide vote divides, as it actually did in 1964, 61.0 per cent for Johnson, 38.4 per cent

---

[2] The statistical technique employed is the parabolic regression, although experiments have also been conducted with (a) linear regressions and (b) weighted means.

[3] The Stalemate Index is defined in Footnote 1 on page 137. By adding the constant 100 to each Stalemate Index, it was possible to produce results so that numbers below 100 could be classified as pro-Republican and those above 100 pro-Democratic.

for Goldwater, and 0.6 per cent for others, the National Stalemate Index is 11.3.[4]

The next step was to add the National Stalemate Index (in this case, 11.3) to the Predicted State Stalemate Index that most nearly produces a sum of 100.0 (in this case, South Carolina's 87.6 plus 11.3 add up to 98.9, whereas Nebraska's 91.0 plus 11.3 amount to 102.3). An "Electoral College cut-off line" is then drawn just *below* the state that produces these results. In 1964, this would have been South Carolina, as shown in the 1964 Forecast column.

Next, tally up the votes of the states *above* the cut-off line; the total represents a predicted Republican Electoral College vote. This predicted outcome, based upon a 61.0-38.4 Democratic-Republican split in the popular vote, would have been 60 Electoral College votes in 1964. Goldwater actually received 52 Electoral College votes. The sum of the state votes *below* the cut-off line would have been 475 for Johnson. Johnson actually received 483 Electoral College votes (not including the District of Columbia's three).

Notice, however, that this illustrative 1964 Electoral College Forecast is based upon the actual 61.0-38.4 popular vote split in 1964. What information do we have *before* Election Day in order to predict the National Stalemate Index we need to fix our Electoral College cut-off point? The answer is the poll findings—Gallup, Roper, and others—as they are reported during the presidential campaign. However, be sure that the poll percentages account for "other candidates," "undecided," etc., in order to produce on over-all 100 per cent for the total electorate.

In 1964 the author used the Gallup Poll report of October 18, which showed the nationwide presidential electorate divided 64.0 per cent for Johnson, 29.0 per cent for Goldwater, and 7.0 per cent "undecided" or for "others." Had the poll been perfect, of course, it would have forecast the 61.0-38.4-0.6 division that actually occurred. Nonetheless, using the Gallup 64.0-29.0 finding to produce a Predicted National Stalemate Index of 17.5, the author located the "Electoral College cut-off point" just below Tennessee (82.6 plus 17.5 add up to 100.1). On this basis, he forecast that Goldwater would receive 28 Electoral College votes (Alabama, Mississippi, and Tennessee) and Johnson 507 (not including D. C.).[5] The actual outcome was, as indicated above, 483-52.

To forecast the 1968 Electoral College outcome, the reader need only add the latest Gallup Poll data to the information in the 1968 Electoral College Forecast column above. This now is an easy do-it-yourself forecast kit.

Step 1: Check the 1968 presidential preference polls for percentages favoring each party nominee, "other party" candidates, and "undecideds." (In our illustration here, we are assuming that the nationwide presidential electorate is split exactly 50-50, with no "other party" or "undecided" preferences.)

[4] From 61.0 subtract 38.4, leaving 22.6. One half of 22.6 is 11.3, the National Stalemate Index. In this election, Goldwater would have had to move his proportion of the vote by 11.3 per cent in order to tie Johnson in popular votes cast.

[5] See report in *San Francisco Examiner,* October 31, 1964.

1964 Electoral College Forecast

Predicted Stalemate Indexes, Ranked	State	Electoral College Vote
70.6	Alabama	10
75.9	Mississippi	7
82.6	Tennessee	11
83.6	Alaska	3
84.5	Oklahoma	8
85.8	Hawaii	4
86.7	Kentucky	9
87.6	So. Carolina	8

cut-off point

91.0	Nebraska	5
91.9	Indiana	13
92.9	Georgia	12
93.4	Missouri	12
93.4	Delaware	3
93.9	Kansas	7
94.5	No. Carolina	13
95.2	Ohio	26
95.4	Pennsylvania	29
95.6	Arizona	5
95.8	So. Dakota	4
95.9	Washington	9
96.0	Oregon	6
96.0	Iowa	9
96.6	Virginia	12
97.5	Colorado	6
97.9	California	40
98.1	West Virginia	7
98.8	Michigan	21
98.9	Arkansas	6
99.6	Wyoming	3
99.6	Illinois	26
99.7	Florida	14
99.9	Utah	4
100.2	Maine	4
100.6	Vermont	3
101.6	New Hampshire	4
103.6	Minnesota	10
104.0	Montana	4
104.5	New Mexico	4
105.6	No. Dakota	4
105.6	New Jersey	17

1968 Electoral College Forecast

Predicted Stalemate Indexes, Ranked	State	Electoral College Vote
71.8	No. Dakota	4
73.6	Mississippi	7
75.4	So. Dakota	4
76.9	Idaho	4
83.2	Nevada	3
83.3	Kansas	7
83.5	Nebraska	5
83.8	So. Carolina	8
87.9	Wyoming	3
89.0	Vermont	3
90.0	Montana	4
90.6	Iowa	9
91.0	Louisiana	10
91.3	Oregon	6
93.4	Wisconsin	12
94.0	California	40
94.2	Arizona	5
94.9	Florida	14
95.9	Virginia	12
96.2	Colorado	6
97.4	Indiana	13
97.7	Maryland	10
97.7	Minnesota	10
98.1	New Mexico	4
99.9	New Hampshire	4

illustrative cut-off point

100.7	Michigan	21
101.0	Illinois	26
101.0	Washington	9
102.1	Massachusetts	14
102.1	Maine	4
103.7	New York	43
103.7	Connecticut	8
103.8	Texas	25
104.1	New Jersey	17
104.6	Alabama	10
104.8	Delaware	3
104.9	Ohio	26
106.2	Pennsylvania	29
106.5	Tennessee	11
106.8	Missouri	12

1964 Electoral College Forecast			*1968 Electoral College Forecast*		
Predicted Stalemate Indexes, Ranked [a]	State	Electoral College Vote [b]	Predicted Stalemate Indexes, Ranked [a]	State	Electoral College Vote
106.0	Idaho	4	107.1	Oklahoma	8
106.0	Wisconsin	12	107.5	Utah	4
107.1	New York	43	108.2	Rhode Island	4
108.0	Maryland	10	108.2	No. Carolina	13
109.7	Nevada	3	109.4	Arkansas	6
110.8	Texas	25	111.0	Georgia	12
111.1	Connecticut	8	111.0	Alaska	3
117.5	Louisiana	10	115.4	West Virginia	7
125.8	Massachusetts	14	116.6	Kentucky	9
129.7	Rhode Island	4	119.5	Hawaii	4

a See text for derivation of Electoral College cut-off point.

b The illustrative cut-off point hypothesizes an exact 50-50 split in popular preferen for only two party nominees in 1968. The 1968 trend projection is based upon four-election analysis of the returns for 1952–1964.

Step 2: Subtract the Republican percentage from the Democrati Divide the answer by two. This produces the National Stalemate Inde (In our illustration here, this Index is zero.)

Step 3: Add the quotient found in Step 2 to the number in the Pr dicted Stalemate Index column that most nearly produces 100.0. (In ou present example, zero added to New Hampshire's 99.9 gets us closest t 100.0.) Draw a line *below* that number and state name to fix the "Elec toral College cut-off point."

Step 4: Add up the Electoral College votes above the line for th Predicted Republican Electoral College vote and below the line for th Democratic. (In the present example, excluding the District of Columbia this produces 207 Electoral College votes for the Republicans and 32 for the Democrats.)

What is most interesting about the Electoral College result of ou hypothetical 50-50 nationwide popular vote split in 1968 is the heav lead enjoyed by the Democrats. Should the number of Democratic an Republican popular votes be the same, the Democrats would still prob ably receive 58 more votes in the Electoral College than they need to wir that is, with 270 Electoral College votes needed to win, the Democrati nominee would probably receive 328 as the result of a 50-50 popula vote split.

Put another way, in order to barely squeak through to victory, th Republicans would need to garner 52 per cent of the popular vote.